THE
GREATEST
COMMANDMENT

Errata

Page 12 "Ra" should be שר
        "vra" should be ישראל
Page 40 "vuvh" should be יהוה
        "hbst" should be אדני
Page 99 The Hebrew above *Al l'vav'cha* should be אל לבבך
Page 125 The first Hebrew word in the title should be קשרתם
Page 133 The Hebrew for *Shaddai* should be שדי
Page 151 The first Hebrew word in the title should be ברכו

THE
GREATEST
COMMANDMENT

*How the Sh'ma Leads to More
Love in Your Life*

IRENE LIPSON

with a Foreword by Daniel Juster, Th.D
Director, Tikkun Ministries International

Lederer Books
a division of
Messianic Jewish Publishers
Clarksville, Maryland

Unless otherwise indicated, Scripture quotations are taken from, and follow the
format of, the *Complete Jewish Bible,* Copyright © 1998 by David H. Stern,
Published by Jewish New Testament Publications, Inc. Used by Permission.

Please note: Dr. Stern numbered verses according to the Jewish bible first, then the
Christian bible, when there is a variance. Also, the CJB often transliterates
the Hebrew word, replacing the traditional English renderings,
where deemed appropriate.

Cover Design by
Josh Huhn, Design Point, Inc.

12 11 10 09 08 07   6 5 4 3 2 1

ISBN 13: 978-1-880226-36-0
ISBN 10: 1-880226-36-7

Library of Congress Control Number: 2007925883
Printed in the United States of America

Lederer Books
a division of
Messianic Jewish Publishers
6120 Day Long Lane
Clarksville, MD 21029

Distributed by
Messianic Jewish Resources International
Order line: (800) 410-7367
E-mail: lederer@messianicjewish.net
Website: www.messianicjewish.net

In Memory of Eric

כִּי-עַזָּה כַמָּוֶת אַהֲבָה
Love is as strong as death.
<small>SONG OF SOLOMON</small> 8:6

CONTENTS

The following abbreviations are used in the text:

Tanakh (Old Covenant):

Genesis (Gen.)

Exodus (Exod.)

Leviticus (Lev.)

Numbers (Num.)

Deuteronomy (Deut.)

Joshua (Josh.)

1 Samuel (1 Sam.)

2 Samuel (2 Sam)

Nehemiah (Neh.)

Psalms (Ps.)

Proverbs (Prov.)

Isaiah (Isa.)

Jeremiah (Jer.)

Ezekiel (Ezek.)

Hosea (Hos.)

Zechariah (Zech.)

Malachi (Mal.)

Brit Chadasha (New Covenant):

Matthew (Matt.)

Acts of the Apostles (Acts)

Romans (Rom.)

I Corinthians (1 Cor.)

2 Corinthians (2 Cor.)

Galatians (Gal.)

Ephesians (Eph.)

Philippians (Phil.)

Colossians (Col.)

2 Timothy (2 Tim)

Hebrews (Heb.)

1 Peter (1 Pet.)

Revelation (Rev.)

Talmud:

First Order: Seeds

Berakhot (Ber.)—Blessings: laws relating to prayer.

Second Order: Seasons

Shabbat (Shab.)—Sabbath: most of the laws governing the Sabbath.

Pesachim (Pes.)—Paschal Offerings: the laws concerning Passover.

Yoma—the Day: concerning *Yom Kippur* (Day of Atonement).

Sukkah (Sukk.)—Booth: concerning the Festival of *Sukkot* (Tabernacles).

Megillah (Meg.)—Scroll: concerning the writing and public reading of Torah, the Prophets, and the scroll of Esther.

Third Order: Women

Nedarim (Ned.)—Vows: laws concerning vows.

Sotah (Sot.)—A woman suspected of adultery: how to deal with such a case; also concerning the Priestly Benediction.

Kiddushin (Kidd.)—Betrothals: laws governing the betrothal relationship.

Fourth Order: Torts

Avot (Av.)—Fathers: a compilation of the sayings of various sages.

Fifth Order: Sanctities

Menahot (Men.)—Meal-offerings: concerning cereal offerings; also concerning *tzitzit* and *tefillin.*

FOREWORD

It was a great pleasure for me to read this book on the Greatest Commandment by Irene Lipson. In the early 1980s I was privileged to meet Eric Lipson. He was a very unusual man; indeed way ahead of his time. For decades he had already put forth a clear Messianic Jewish theology and was committed to the importance of all the gifts of the Holy Spirit. Previously he had served as a Reform Rabbi. He was as dear a man as one could imagine. His combination of Jewish knowledge and Yeshua centered Jewish piety was deeply impressive.

What I did not know then, was that his wife Irene was in her own right a significant thinker and had deep understanding and commitment to the same values and perspective.

In this very wonderful little book, we find a very fine outline of both Jewish traditional teaching on the Sh'ma and re-application from a New Covenant perspective. The book yields good knowledge, but much more shows a deep devotional quality. It is a great example of what I would like to see as the Jewish expression of New Covenant commitment. We enter Jewish space when we open the pages of this book. We enter the power of the New Covenant as well. It is integrated.

This is not just a book on the commandment itself, but on the whole of what was accepted in Jewish tradition as part of the Sh'ma liturgical readings, Deuteronomy 6, 11 and Numbers 15. The preliminary blessings before and the subsequent blessing after the Sh'ma are also included in her treatment. Thus we find helpful interpretation on the fringes, the tallit, and on tifillin. We find good material on the education of children, both in the family and in the community.

I have concluded that all who read this book will find blessing and will be glad for their effort.

Daniel Juster
Director, Tikkun Ministries International
First President, Union of Messianic Jewish Congregations

The Sh'ma

שְׁמַע יִשְׂרָאֵל יהוה אֱלֹהֵינוּ יהוה אֶחָד

"Sh'ma Yisra'el! ADONAI Eloheynu, ADONAI echad.
Hear, O Isra'el, the LORD our God, the LORD is one" (Deut. 6:4).

(בָּרוּךְ שֵׁם כְּבוֹד מַלְכוּתוֹ לְעוֹלָם וָעֶד)

(Baruch shem k'vod malkhooto l'olam va'ed.)
(Blessed be his name whose glorious kingdom is forever and ever.)

And you are to love ADONAI your God with all your heart, all your being and all your resources. These words, which I am ordering you today, are to be on your heart; and you are to teach them carefully to your children. You are to talk about them when you sit at home, when you are traveling on the road, when you lie down and when you get up. Tie them on your hand as a sign, put them at the front of a headband around your forehead, and write them on the door-frames of your house and on your gates (Deut. 6:5–9)

So if you listen carefully to my mitzvot which I am giving you today, to love ADONAI your God and serve him with all your heart and all your being; then I will give your land its rain at the right seasons, including the early fall rains and the late spring rains; so that you can gather in your wheat, new wine and olive oil; and I will give your fields grass for your livestock; with the result that you will eat and be satisfied. But be careful not to let yourselves be seduced, so that you turn aside, serving other gods and worshipping them. If you do, the anger of ADONAI will blaze up against you. He will shut up the sky, so that there will be no rain. The ground will not yield its produce, and you will quickly pass away from the good land ADONAI is giving you. Therefore, you are to store up these words of mine in your heart and in all your being; tie them on your hand as a sign; put them at the front of a headband around your forehead; teach them carefully to your children, talking about them when you sit at home, when you are traveling on the road, when you lie down and when you get up; and write them on the door-frames of your house and on your gates–so that you and your children will live long on the land ADONAI swore to your ancestors that he would give them for as long as there is sky above the earth. (Deut. 11:13–21)

ADONAI said to Moshe, "Speak to the people of Isra'el, instructing them to make, through all their generations, *tzitziyot* on the corners of their garments, and to put with the *tzitzit* on each corner a blue thread. It is to be a *tzitzit* for you to look at and thereby remember all of ADONAI's mitzvot and obey them, so that you won't go around wherever your own heart and eyes lead you to prostitute yourselves; but it will help you remember and obey all my mitzvot and be holy for your God. I am ADONAI your God, who brought you out of the land of Egypt in order to be your God. I am ADONAI your God." (Num. 15:37–41)

Introducing the *Sh'ma*

God wants us to love him.

God desires, above all else, that his people should love him—totally, unconditionally, unreservedly. How, though, can we love someone we do not know? Love at first sight may be exciting, exhilarating, but it is built on a shallow foundation and may not last. It is as we get to know a person that we are able to build a relationship in which love may grow. The Bible describes the man-woman love relationship as "knowing" (Gen. 4:1).

God has made himself known to us in many ways. It is, however, in the first words of the Sh'ma that we find perhaps the most concise expression of who he is both in eternity and in relation to his people. Only after laying down the rich soil of that declaration does he command us to grow and nourish the flowering of love for him.

In these three passages from the Torah (Pentateuch) we see the God of Isra'el presenting himself to his people. He says, in effect, "This is who I am. Remember what I have done for you, how I have loved you. I want you to know me and love me in return. Soak yourself in my words so that you may know me better. This is how you will cultivate your relationship with me; and here are some things you can do to nurture your love, to guard against complacency, forgetfulness, and idolatry."

In this book we shall explore the Sh'ma, not as a theological exercise, nor as an historical curiosity. I pray that together we may embark on a journey of discovery—about who God is; how much he has loved us; how we may learn to know and love him better. O that we may truly come to love him with all our heart, being, and resources.

Who, then, is this God?

The First Principle of the Jewish Faith

The first of Maimonides' thirteen principles states:

> I believe with perfect faith that the Creator, blessed be his name, is the Author and Guide of everything that has been created, and that he alone has made, does make, and will make all things.

All the Jewish traditions agree on this one matter: that the Sh'ma (Hear, O Isra'el...) occupies the supreme place in Jewish thought, tradition, and theology. Maimonides, the great mediaeval philosopher, expresses in this, the first of his principles of faith, the primal and fundamental declaration of Isra'el's faith. There is a God; he is unique; this God alone is the cause and fount of all Creation. The Sh'ma's importance is reinforced by the fact that the Talmud itself opens with the question: "From what time may one recite the Sh'ma in the evening?" (*Ber.* 1:2a). The rabbis have taught that the opening sentence of the Sh'ma occupies the central place in Jewish religious thought. Everything else in Judaism springs from these words. Every belief, every practice, revolves around the hub of this proclamation that God is the Lord, that he has a special relationship with Isra'el, and that he is unique.

This credal statement is not only words for us to accept and believe. We are to speak those words—aloud. How else can anyone obey the command to "hear"? The opening sentence is the earliest prayer learned by infants, the last confession of the dying. It has been "the watchword and rallying-cry of a hundred generations in Israel" (Hertz, *A Book of Jewish Thoughts* 196). The rabbis have taught that a man is diminished if he fails to observe the commandment concerning the Sh'ma: "Who is an *am ha'aretz* (man of the earth, unspiritual man)?" Anyone who does not recite the Sh'ma evening and morning—this is the view of R. Eliezer" (*Ber.* 47b). Among adult men, only the bridegroom on his wedding night is exempt. Rabbi Gamaliel, however, who was the grandson of Hillel, a leading Rabbi of the first century C.E., refused to take advantage of this exemption, declaring, "I will not...remove from myself the kingship of heaven even for a moment" (*Ber.* 16a).

Affirmation of the unity of God and the requirement to love and obey him in response has been the throbbing life-force within

Judaism. These words are "Judaism's highly charged assertion of God's oneness, of God's covenant faithfulness to Israel, his people, and their commitment to him alone, followed by the recognition that he is also the One God of all creation" (Nanos, 180–81).

Declaration of the first line of the Sh'ma is also an act of testimony. It is usual to enlarge the first and last letters (*'ayin* and *dalet*), which together form the word *'ed*. That is the Hebrew word for "witness." As we say the familiar words we are bearing *witness* to the only true God. We are declaring ourselves to be his people. That is who we are. This is our "collective self-expression" (Hertz, *Authorised Daily Prayer Book with Commentary* 266).

Judaism's Credo

The first sentence of the Sh'ma sums up the teaching of the first two commandments. These words are the nearest Judaism gets to a credal statement. There are some variations in the way they are translated. *Rashbam*, the twelfth century Bible exegete, favored "Hear, O Israel, the Lord is our God, the Lord alone"; Hertz preferred "Hear, O Israel: the Lord is our God, the Lord is One" (Hertz, *Deuteronomy* 83). Hertz's version is more commonly accepted today. This verse has been a watchword, a confession of faith, from very early times:

> It [The Sh'ma] is said when one is praising God and when one is beseeching Him. The faithful Jew says it even when questioning Him. The Sh'ma is said when our lives are full of hope, it is said when all hope is gone and the end is near. Whether in moments of joy or despair, in thankfulness or in resignation, it is the expression of Jewish conviction, the historic proclamation of Judaism's central creed. (Donin, 144)

The three paragraphs that comprise the whole Sh'ma are, however, more than a simple declaration of belief. They incorporate a demand of personal response—primarily of love. Love, in its turn, requires allegiance, and obedience to certain mitzvot (commands). It has always been a tenet of Judaism that doing is of more value than believing. We demonstrate our love by the things that we do, the way we conduct ourselves.

The Yoke of the Kingdom of Heaven

The rabbis have defined the recital of the Sh'ma as "the acceptance of the yoke of the Kingdom of Heaven" (*Ber.*, 13a). Cohen describes this acceptance as an act of submission to divine discipline (Cohen 4). Opinions have differed as to how much of the Sh'ma is required to constitute this acceptance. Is it just the first sentence, as *Yehudah HaNasi*, the redactor of the *Mishnah* (the basis of Talmud), thought (*Ber.* 13b)? Is it the first section? Is it all three sections? Perhaps the most helpful way of looking at the matter is in *B'rakhot* 14b: "First he accepts the yoke of the Kingdom of Heaven and he accepts the yoke of the commandments." The consensus seems to be that if a man dons the *tefillin* (phylacteries), then recites the Sh'ma, and then offers his prayers, he has truly taken upon himself the yoke of the Kingdom of Heaven.

In History

It seems likely that the Sh'ma did consist, originally, of just the one verse—Deuteronomy 6:4. Over the centuries, however, it has come to include the three passages shown at the beginning of this book. This custom was already established before the compilation of the Mishnah. It is believed that Moses intended the second paragraph specifically to be included in the public reading of Torah enjoined in Deuteronomy 31:11. As for the third section, Mishnah records an early discussion about the importance of mentioning the Exodus from Egypt in the recitation of the Sh'ma (Ber. 12b). The rabbis were concerned to make a connection between belief and action. In reciting the first paragraph, one is accepting the yoke of the Kingdom of heaven; in the second and third paragraphs, one is accepting the yoke of the mitzvot (Plaut, 1407). Friedlander states categorically that the twice-daily reading of all three passages is assumed in the Mishnah as being already established by law and by usage (Friedlander, 431). The reading of the whole three sections is called *K'riat* (Reciting) *Sh'ma*.

There is a tradition that Moshe (Moses), in his farewell address, commanded the twice daily recitation of the Sh'ma. It has even been thought that the custom dates back to the time of Jacob. Certainly, the practice seems to go as far back as the return from exile, under the authority of Ezra. By this morning and evening recitation, so the thinking goes, one fulfills the injunction to meditate on these words day and night (Josh. 1:8). Some have tried, over the years, to substitute or add other passages in the liturgy, but nothing has come of such attempts. The Sh'ma has a unique hold over the people of Isra'el; it is unrivaled in their affections and loyalties.

It is the first sentence that has particularly stirred the soul of Jews through the centuries, becoming a symbol to Jewish people of courage, hope, and commitment. Most famously, these words were on the lips of Rabbi Akiba, the first century C.E. father of Rabbinical Judaism, as he was being tortured to death. It was as if his life reached its climax of faith at that point. Many Jewish martyrs have followed in this tradition. The poet Kalonymos ben Yehudah wrote, during the time of the Crusades:

Yea, they slay us and they smite,
Vex our souls with sore afright;
All the closer cleave we, LORD,
To Thine everlasting word.
Not a line of all their Mass
Shall our lips in homage pass;
Though they curse, and bind, and kill,
The living God is with us still.
We still are Thine, though limbs are torn;
Better death than life forsworn.
From dying lips the accents swell,
'Thy God is One, O Israel';
And bridegroom answers unto bride,
'The LORD is God, and none beside,'
And, knit with bonds of holiest faith,
They pass to endless life through death.
(Hertz, *Deuteronomy* 107)

During times of persecution, and there have been many, Jewish people have used the Sh'ma as a sort of password—a sign of identity. The story is that in Auschwitz a medallion inscribed with these words was passed round as a signal to activate the failed revolt. During World War Two, many Jewish children were taken into Christian homes and institutions. There was appreciation for kindness and courage shown, but of course after the war there was a desire to reclaim these children to their own inheritance. Searchers for surviving Jewish children toured the European monasteries and convents reciting the words of the Sh'ma. Those children who responded were rescued for the Jewish community wherever possible.

Three Sections

After the first six words, the first section of the Sh'ma emphasizes basic religious responsibilities. We are to love God; to teach his words to our children; to talk about his words; to lay tefillin; to place *mezuzot* (boxes containing the Shema and other scriptures) on the doors of our homes and the gates of our cities.

The second section is more practical. It is about the application of the principles stated in the first section. It deals with issues of reward and punishment. God will bless his people if they obey his commandments, so that they will enjoy life in their own land. He will withhold his blessing if they do not. God gives his people a choice, but our success as his people depends upon our obedience to his will. Donin suggests that whereas the first section is addressed to the individual Jew, the second is directed to the collective body of Isra'el (Donin, 151). This principle of reward and punishment is enshrined in Maimonides' eleventh principle: "He, the exalted one, rewards him who obeys the commands of the Torah, and punishes him who transgresses its prohibitions" (Jacobs, *Principles of the Jewish Faith* 350).

The third section deals primarily with the putting of *tzitziyot* (fringes or tassels) on one's garment. The purpose of these is to remind us of God's commandments, that we may remember and be helped to obey them, thus demonstrating our love for him.

Evening and Morning

One should recite the Sh'ma before sleeping at night. This is a private, personal act. It ensures that one keeps short accounts with

God, and that one goes to sleep with the words of Torah in mind. It is one of the five fixed daily orders of prayer. It should also be the last words on the lips of the dying. Telushkin tells a story about this, relating to a man who hung a bell in the back of his car. Why did he do that?

> When I drive on the road . . . and I hit a bump, the bell tinkles. That tinkle reminds me that there are mitzvot I can fulfill just by thinking about them. . . . And if, God forbid, I suddenly lose control of the car . . . the last sound I will hear will be the tinkle of the bell, and I'll be reminded to say, 'Sh'ma Yisra'el, Adonai Eloheinu, Adonai Ekhad.' At least that way, I'll leave this world with a blessing, rather than a curse. (Telushkin, 358)

The morning recital should be the first act of the day proper, when there is an appreciable amount of light. When it is a congregational act, the requirement is to do it worshipfully. According to the teaching of the rabbis, God promises that when his people gather together and recite the Sh'ma as one, with *kavannah* (reverent intention), he and his angels will listen to them.

For Protection

Reading the Sh'ma on one's bed supposedy gave protection. Rabbi Isaac claimed that "It is as though he holds a two-edged sword in his hand"; evil spirits, it seemed, would flee at the sound of the words (*Ber.* 5a). It gives the power to resist temptation. If a man could defeat the *yetzer ha rah* (evil impulse) said R. Levi ben Hama in the name of R. Simeon ben Lakish, "Let him study the Torah. . . If he subdues it, well and good. If not, let him recite the Sh'ma" (*Ber.* 5a).

One rabbi, unnamed, even encouraged impious men: "I care not what deed of impiety you do; but perform for me one request: say the Sh'ma daily." There is a Hasidic tradition that many followed his advice and became men of faith. Newman comments: "It is a comforting lesson to those sinners who recite the Sh'ma that through its power they may escape perdition!" (Newman, 334–35)

A Way of Praying

The Sh'ma is not a prayer in the usual sense of the word, but it has for centuries been an integral part of the liturgical service. Even though it addresses us and not God, Jewry regards it as a prayer because of its unique power to "bring the life of the Torah into our everyday world" (Rossel, 155). Indeed, the earliest forms of liturgical prayer probably consisted only of the Sh'ma and the blessings following. It is good to discipline oneself to order one's thoughts biblically before launching into prayer itself. That, no doubt, is why the rabbis who compiled the Mishnah began the tractate on prayer (*B'rakhot*) with the question about the reading of the Sh'ma.

In Usage

One may recite the Sh'ma in any language (*Sot.* 32a), sitting or standing, though the usual custom is to stand and to use Hebrew. One must speak the words correctly, and with kavannah. Tradition has it that Yehudah HaNasi, leader of the Sanhedrin in Isra'el in the third century C.E., covered his face when reciting the first verse. This is common practice today; the purpose being to promote concentration. One may also meditate briefly in silence before beginning to speak the words. Maimonides taught that one should make a real effort to empty one's mind beforehand.

For Believers in Yeshua (Jesus)

Yeshua was certainly familiar with the Sh'ma. He quoted from it when asked which was the greatest or most important *mitzvah* (commandment). "You are to love ADONAI [the LORD] your God with all your heart and with all your soul and with all your strength," came the reply. Then he added, as the second most important, a quotation from Leviticus 19:18: "You are to love your neighbor as yourself" (Matt. 22:39). Sha'ul (Paul) seems to have based some of his argument in the letter to the Romans on at least the first sentence of the Sh'ma. As God is One, the only God, he must of course be God of the Gentiles as well as the Jews!

Messianic Jews recite these words for several reasons. We wish to show solidarity with Isra'el, to make the statement: "We are still Jews." More than that, we want to *feel* our Jewishness within ourselves in a meaningful, biblical way. We want to discover and explore the background which so many have lost, either having been raised as secular Jews or having conformed to gentile forms of worship.

Surely, it is of value for all believers in Yeshua to consider these words. Jewish people particularly sometimes accuse us of being polytheists—of worshipping three gods. We do not. Christians can proclaim, with Isra'el, "The Lord is our God, the Lord is one."

There is an important lesson in the Sh'ma for all of us. Faith begins with belief that there is a God—but this alone is not enough. It is necessary to be in relationship with that God. He wishes to be "our" God, "my" God. More than that—what he has done for us calls for a response of love. Love without action is empty. Real love leads to action, to a life lived in obedience to his will, as revealed in the Scriptures—his Word. These are the principles enshrined in the Sh'ma.

In this book, we are going to take the Sh'ma, section by section, and consider what it says to us today. To some, the practices described will be familiar. Do you, though, know *why* you do these things? We will make them more spiritually meaningful. To others they might perhaps seem weird, foreign, utterly irrelevant. Give yourself a chance to be surprised!

I come to you as one who identifies with both groups, as one who is a gentile by birth, a believer in Messiah Yeshua by new birth, and a Messianic Jew by marriage. I have been enriched beyond words as, through thirty-four years of marriage to a Jewish believer in Yeshua, I discovered some of the many treasures embedded in Jewish teaching and custom. That means that, in this book, you will find me sometimes identifying with Isra'el and at other times with the Christian Church. I hope you will not find that bewildering. It is simply my way of working out the concept of the "one new man" in Yeshua.

As we understand a little more about God's dealings with Isra'el, we may, we just may, begin to discover more about what he is like and how he wants to relate to us all.

A Call
To Listen

CHAPTER 1

Hear

שְׁמַע

Sh'ma

It is important that the Sh'ma be recited audibly. The Talmud clearly directs that the command to "hear" can only be obeyed if there is something to which to listen: "One who recites the Sh'ma must do so audibly, as it says, Hear, O Israel...which implies: 'Let thine ear hear what thy mouth utters'" (*Meg.* 20a). It is not enough to mutter the Sh'ma under one's breath.

Hearing, however, is not only something we do with our ears. There is an inner listening too. "When thou hearest bear in mind that thy power of hearing comes from thy soul," taught the Besht (Ba'al Shem Tov), an eighteenth century rabbi, founder of the Hasidic movement (Newman, 511). This means that the hearing implied by the first word of the Sh'ma is to be a response of the whole personality. Letting words "go in one ear and out the other" is not listening-hearing. The Hebrew verb signifies letting words sink in, thinking about them, understanding them. We sometimes use the expression "I hear what you are saying, meaning, "I understand what you are saying." The prophet Mikhah (Micah) called his people back to God, urging them to "listen" in order to "remember" and "understand" (Mic. 6:1–5). In terms of the Sh'ma, the great foundation statement of Jewish belief, the worshiper uses this word to call himself to an attitude of paying careful attention to what follows. We say the words aloud, not only so that others may hear, but also so that we may ourselves hear and respond. We have truly heard only if we intend in our hearts to act on the words. "On the intention of the heart depends the validity of the words" (*Ber.* 15a).

The Voice of God

We have a choice about who, and what, we hear. Should we listen to the voice of the world, of the culture that surrounds us? Should we open our minds to those who say that right is wrong, and wrong is right? No, says Mikhah again. "Listen to the rod and to him who commissioned it," not to those who hold sway in society, who "tell lies, with tongues of deceit in their mouths" (Mic. 6:9–12). The prevailing culture of our times speaks with the voice of men, not of God. It speaks of reason, not revelation. It is better to hear God's rebuke than man's more comfortable lies.

It is God to whom we must open our ears, and not only in the recitation of the Sh'ma. The Talmud teaches that God is speaking all the time, if we will only listen. "Every day a divine voice goes forth from Mount Horeb," said Rabbi Joshua ben Levi (*Ber.* 17b). The implication is that God still speaks today. His words never date, never grow irrelevant. Whoever we are, whatever time and space we inhabit, he speaks right into our situation. We are the losers if we do not listen.

Listen and Do

Listening means thinking and understanding. It means even more than that. There has to be a positive acceptance of what is heard. This means faith. Faith in its turn, must involve obedience. A true hearer of God will be living a committed and obedient life. "Listen, Isra'el, and take care to obey" was Moshe's instruction immediately before the Sh'ma (Deut. 6:3). At the foot of Sinai, near the beginning of the great adventure, the people had made a promise: "Everything that ADONAI has spoken, we will do [*naaseh*] and obey [*nishma*]" (Exod. 24:7). There is a section in the *midrash* that explains why Moshe used the word "Sh'ma" in his final teaching. It says that God betrothed Isra'el to himself with two precious jewels: *naaseh* and *nishma*. The Israelites lost one of these jewels—*naaseh*—when they made the golden calf; so Moshe wanted them to take care not to lose the other jewel—*nishma* (*Deut. Rabbah* 3:11). They had failed to "do," but there was hope if they would at least "listen."

Listen and Give Heed

The words of the Sh'ma are not intended to be only a recitation by rote. We are to ponder, study, and comprehend them. So it is with the lessons of life and of history. Yesha'yahu (Isaiah) asked the question, "Who will hear and give heed in the times to come?" (Isa. 42:23). The great historic event of Isra'el's history is the Exodus—our national redemption from slavery in Egypt. What do we learn from that—about God, about ourselves? For believers in Yeshua the great historic event is the death on the cross of the sin-bearing Messiah, followed by his Resurrection—our personal redemption from slavery to sin. What do we learn from that—about God, about ourselves? Hirsch counseled Isra'el to learn from her national experience as well as from Torah, to take to heart all that life teaches (Hirsch, 5). As individuals we may do the same. Learn the lesson, child of God, from your personal experience. Listen, ponder, and learn. Sh'ma!

Hearing and Seeing

There is a belief that hearing is more meritorious than seeing. Plaut points out that in the beginning Isra'el's faith rested on seeing. The people saw the miracles leading up to Passover night. They saw what God did on that night. They saw the manna, the water from the rock. They saw the cloud and the fire of the Sh'khinah, the manifestations at Sinai. Since that time, however, Isra'el has depended largely on tradition rather than on phenomena which can be seen. That is why the command is to "Hear, O Israel" (Plaut, 1372).

Lamm has another explanation. He suggests that seeing may lead to idolatry, to the creation of icons that represent and attempt to recreate the experience. Hearing is safer. It leads directly to obedience, with no visual forms to distract the worshiper (Lamm, 13).

It is interesting that Yeshua had a word about this. Thomas demanded visual and tangible proof of the Resurrection. Yeshua graciously met him in the place of doubt where he was floundering, but with a gentle admonishment: "Have you trusted because you have seen me? How blessed are those who do not see, but trust anyway!" (John 20:29). Honest doubts, there may be. Nevertheless, we are to hear and respond with obedience and commitment, even when we do not see or understand.

Refusal to Listen

God warned Yesha'yahu that he would not be listened to, that he should tell the people, "Yes, you hear, but you don't understand" (Isa. 6:9). There is even the implication that if people persist in not listening, God himself will "stop up their ears" and cut off the possibility of repentance (Isa. 6:10). Later, the prophet seemed to have these words in mind when, in exasperation, he pronounced, "You open your ears, but you don't listen" (Isa. 42:20). Yirmeyahu (Jeremiah) had the same experience: "I spoke to you again and again, but you wouldn't listen" (Jer. 7:13). The cry came again and again through the ages: "Hear the word of the Lord, O House of Isra'el."

Moshe knew all about not being heard. At the end of his life, he reminded the people: "I told you, but you wouldn't listen." The result of that rebellion at Kadesh-Barnea, and the subsequent disaster, was that when they returned and cried to the Lord, he neither listened to what they said nor paid them any attention (Deut. 1:43–45). Now there is an awesome thought: If we will not listen to God when he chooses to speak, he just might not listen to us when we eventually choose to respond!

That is never the last word, however. There is always the possibility of returning and listening. "For ADONAI your God is a merciful God. He will not fail you, destroy you, or forget the covenant with your ancestors which he swore to them" (Deut. 4: 31). Nevertheless, the way back can be hard and long (v. 30). Better to listen the first time he speaks.

So important was this issue of listening, that God set before the people a blessing and a curse. The blessing was to be theirs if they listened to him in the days to come; the curse would come upon them if they did not. He even told them to "put the blessing on Mount G'rizim and the curse on Mount 'Eival" (Deut. 11:29). That would serve as a visual reminder.

Listen, Listen

Sometimes the word is repeated, as in Exodus 15:26. At the beginning of Isra'el's journey, the word was forceful: "Listen, listen." This repetition is for reinforcement: "Listen *intently.*"

The rabbis have a delightful explanation for this duplication. It is that if I choose to hear, God reinforces my ability to hear. He will even enable me to hear for the rest of my life. "So, if a man hearkens to one command, God gives him the power to hearken to many" (Montefiore, 198).

Yeshua

Given the importance of the command to "hear," it is not surprising that at the Transfiguration, that supreme moment of the affirmation of Yeshua's identity, the words the three *talmidim* (disciples) heard were, "This is my Son, whom I love, with whom I am well pleased. Listen to him!" (Matt. 17:5). Luke records it as "This is my Son, whom I have chosen. Listen to him!" (Luke 9:35). Just as Isra'el had been taught to listen—because God is unique, so the followers of Yeshua are to listen to *him*—because *he* is unique.

Yeshua believed in the importance of listening. In echoes of Yesha'yahu, he said, "If you have ears, then hear!" (Matt. 11:15). The signs pointed to his Messiahship, if only they would read those signs; in other words, if only they would listen. Indeed, Matthew later records that Yeshua actually quoted Yesha'yahu on this subject. "I have to talk to them in parables," he said, "because I know that their hearts are set not to listen, not to understand, not to repent and return" (Matt. 13:10–15). With echoes of Rabbi Eliezer's comment about the *am ha'aretz* (see Introduction), he spoke strong words about listening to God. "Whoever belongs to God listens to what God says; the reason you don't listen is that you don't belong to God" (John 8:47). Strong words indeed.

For Yeshua, as for the rabbis, listening alone was not enough. Hearing had to bear results. Some of his words sing in our ears like music. There are, indeed, people who enjoy listening to them yet have no belief in him and no intention of following him. We are not just to enjoy the sound of his words. We must take note of them, let them impact our lives. In other words, hearing should lead to trust: "Whoever hears what I am saying and trusts the one who sent me has eternal life" (John 5:24). That trust must, in turn, lead to obedient action. He told the parable of the house built on rock and that built on sand to illustrate that hearing should lead to action, to obedience (Matt. 7:24–27).

Sha'ul picked up the thought that hearing is linked to understanding. In his discussion about Isra'el's current rejection of Yeshua as *Mashiach* (Messiah), he said, "Isn't it rather that they didn't hear? No. they did hear…isn't it rather that Isra'el didn't understand?" (Rom. 10:18–19). Sha'ul was saying that many in Isra'el simply had not paid attention to the Good News, not obeyed it, not trusted what they had heard (v. 16).

For Thought

We live in a noisy world. Most of us find it difficult to shut out that noise and hear the voice of ADONAI. There are so many voices. Which one is truly his? I am writing this chapter in the middle of an election campaign in England. Each time I switch on the television I see faces I do not trust, and hear words I do not believe. So what do I do? I switch off the set! The issue is trust. When God speaks, however, the words are believable, because the speaker is trustworthy. Do the words I am listening to match up with the character of a holy God, with the words I can read in the Scriptures? That is how we may know who is speaking. The answer is not to switch off, but to learn and practice discernment.

With advancing years I find it increasingly difficult to hear what people are saying. The problem is particularly acute when there is background noise. This past weekend, I was in conversation with a visitor during the social time after the worship service. There were other conversations going on around us. In addition there was a 'musical' contribution from a small child behind me experimenting on the drums! Many older readers, whose hearing is not what it once was, will know exactly what I am talking about. In such circumstances I find I have to concentrate hard and *look at* the person's face. So it is with listening to God. Sometimes it is really hard work and requires concentration.

There are times when I speak to my seven-year old grandson and he takes not a bit of notice, because his mind is on something else. I have to go and stand in front of him, calling him by name and saying, "Look at me. *Look at me.*" Only when I have established eye-contact will he 'hear' what I am saying. It works the other way, as well. The three year old has been known to pull his mother's face round to him, to ensure he has her full attention!

Sometimes it is difficult to listen to God because of the clamor of inner turmoil, distracting circumstances, painful situations, decisions that have to be made, or problems tackled. Maimonides' counsel is helpful here: we need to exercise the will and deliberately clear the mind of these distractions, which are all-absorbing. I find it helps to name them and lay them down one by one. For some, writing them down and then tearing up the paper may be effective. We all function differently, and have to find our own coping mechanisms. Find them we must, or we shall not be able to "listen, listen." Sometimes the walk with the Lord is one of discipline. If you fail the first time, do not give up. Keep at it and you will succeed.

Another helpful technique is to use the Psalms to quiet the spirit and focus the mind. There is something in this book for every situation. For instance, when I have felt absolutely alone and about to spiral down into depression, I have turned to Psalm 3: "But you, ADONAI, are a shield for me; you are my glory, you lift my head high." I contemplate those words, picture in my mind God's *Shekinah* surrounding me, pause and contemplate that reality. I do it again and again, not just once, until peace and joy return. It works. Sometimes everything seems to be going wrong and life is apparently unraveling. Look at Psalm 84:

> Blessed are those whose strength is in you,
> who have set their hearts on pilgrimage.
> As they pass through the valley of Baca [dryness],
> they make it a place of springs. (NIV)

This may be a dry place; I may be weak and helpless, but in the strength of the Lord I will turn it into a fertile field.

We do our children a service if we teach them to listen. Eli the priest, with all his faults, at least got that right (1 Sam. 3:4–10)! If they do not learn to listen to us, how will they learn to listen to God? Listening is a habit. It can be taught, practiced, learned.

So, drop the toys; park the trucks; put down the book; switch off the television set; mute the phone. Turn away from them for a while. Give the Lord your full attention. You really do not want to miss what he is saying to you. Listen. *Sh'ma*!

A Prayer

"My soul waits in silence for God alone" (Ps. 62:1). Lord, I am not very good at waiting in silence. I need help to become a listener. How can I follow you, obey you, be like you, if I don't hear what you are saying to me? So teach me please; teach me the art of silence. Train me in the discipline of concentration. I submit myself to you, to re-learn patterns of listening, of giving you my full attention. Then, Lord, show me how to translate hearing into obedience, into action.

Blessed are you, O Lord our God, King of the universe, who graciously speaks to each one of your people. You are trustworthy, and your words are true and relevant. You are gracious, and your words come to me wrapped in your mercy and love. Blessed are you, who speaks to my heart.

CHAPTER 2

Isra'el

יִשְׂרָאֵל

Yisra'el

The Sh'ma is before all else God's word to Isra'el. It begins with
the command that Isra'el should listen to him. It concludes with
the words "I am ADONAI your God, who brought you out of the
land of Egypt in order to be your God. I am ADONAI your God." It
expresses a relationship with obligations on both sides: Isra'el for
her part will fulfill certain obligations that God does not require of
other nations; she will be his people. God for his part will be faithful to his covenant promise; he will be Isra'el's God. It is this assurance of relationship that has preserved Isra'el's identity
throughout her troubled history.

Calling to Isra'el (*Ya'akov* / Jacob)

There is a tradition that the words, "Hear O Isra'el, the Lord is our
God, the Lord is One," go back to the time of the patriarch Isra'el
and his sons. Lamm suggests that we can view the Sh'ma as Isra'el
the people calling out to Isra'el the patriarch across "the chasm of
the generations," assuring him that the God he worshipped is our
God too. Isra'el can rest in peace, knowing that his descendants
continue the tradition that he entrusted to his own children. The
ages of suffering have not broken Isra'el. More than three and a half
millennia have passed since she first received these words, but "we
still carry aloft our grandfather's torch of *Yihud Hashem* (the unity
of his name)." Even in today's climate of "cynicism, confusion and
despair," Isra'el continues to keep faith (Lamm, 21).

    Genesis, Chapter 32, tells us of the pivotal moment in *Ya'akov's*
life. Here was a "heel-grasper" who felt himself weak, morally and

physically, before the might of his brother Esau. After his encounter with God at Peniel he emerged physically weakened, but spiritually strong because he had confronted God, taken hold, and refused to let go. The runner took a stand at last, as he faced up to himself and the consequences of his actions. The struggle left its mark, but Ya'akov emerged transformed as Isra'el. He was now a different person; limping humility had replaced arrogance and deceit. The grasper of power had become the *sar*—the prince—before God, "bearing witness by his name 'Israel' that 'God is Prince' and Master of all" (Hirsch, 174). What he had previously grasped by cunning and deceit is now his by right—by gift of God. This is what it means to be "Isra'el."

The Name Isra'el

The name "Isra'el" has been given more than one meaning, based on two different ways of interpreting the root of the word. Ra (*sar*) means captain, ruler, prince; vra (*sarah*) means to persist, to persevere. יִשְׂרָאֵל (*Isra'el*) therefore can mean "He who persevered, or, who has striven with God"; "a prince, or champion, of God"; "God is ruler"; "ruling with God." Whichever interpretation we favor, what we have is the indisputable fact that Ya'akov-Isra'el is now on the winning side—God's side. This champion, however, did not achieve his status through his own strength or skill, but by God's grace; the limp bears witness to that. He may have come to this point successful and self-assured, a self-made man. He is now a man with a weakness that the entire world can see. He is not the man he was. He is no longer his own man—God's name is embedded in his own, and will be in that of the generations to come.

The Community of Isra'el

The word *Sh'ma* is singular. It does not address a multitude of individuals acting independently, but a people as a whole. As Jewish people recite the words, either alone or in the congregation, they are aware of doing so as a part of the whole body of Isra'el. The concept of *K'lal Yisra'el* (the whole community of Isra'el) is of tremendous importance. Isra'el is a people alive today. Isra'el is also a people reaching back into the past and forward into the future. It is the visible witness to a God who is faithful. We must not fail our forefathers or our children's children.

This concept of the people as a single person is brought out in a *midrash* on the Tabernacle: "All *Isra'el* is to become unified as if one person whose collective body is represented by the Tabernacle and whose collective spirit consists of the souls of all Jews collected therein" (*Malbim Truma*. Cited by Levine 143).

The rabbis have always laid great importance on Isra'el's duty to proclaim the oneness of God. Why did God honor Isra'el by giving her Torah? Surely, they have said, so that she might be a light to the nations in the declaration that there is only one God. It is, therefore, important that Isra'el stands firmly together as one in affirming this truth. Her oneness witnesses to God's oneness.

Isra'el always stands poised between history and destiny. History reveals a people who have survived by the skin of their teeth a horrendous series of persecutions dating back to the founding Fathers in Egypt. Today we see a people still reeling from history, still in survival mode: "Masada shall not fall again." All this has to be taken on board as Isra'el faces her destiny. The preservation of Isra'el has been for a purpose not yet seen, but hinted at in the words "a light to the nations." God is still "our God"; Isra'el is still "his people." She will yet make the quantum leap from survival mode to purpose mode. Only as God's people can this happen. "Learn the lesson, Isra'el, from your national experience" (Hirsch, 5).

The Members of Isra'el

At the same time, the private affirmation of each individual is an ingredient of the faith of all Isra'el. "He is the God not merely of the past generations, but of all generations, and of every individual soul in each generation" (Hertz, *Exodus* 211). As each Jew declares faith, joining in the recitation of the Sh'ma, he integrates into something that is more than the sum of its parts. If one member breaks faith, Isra'el is less than whole.

Each Jewish person is a child of the patriarch, with a responsibility to identify with the transformed Ya'akov-Isra'el. *I* will never feel at home because Ya'akov's story is *my* story. "Ya'akov-Israel was a wanderer to the end of his life, first as a fugitive, then as a servant in Laban's household and lastly as a shepherd-sheikh. He dies in a foreign land" (Jocz, 238). This is the Jewish experience.

Ya'akov-Isra'el became a man apart; Isra'el is a people apart. The Israelite cannot escape this "different-ness." A remnant has survived which bears God's princely title. God has yet a purpose for this remnant, and each individual Jewish person has a share in that destiny.

The Holy One of Isra'el

Holiness implies "otherness" as well as absolute purity. The prophets, particularly Yesha'yahu, describe God as holy because he is not only good; he is also totally different. We see that "different ness" most clearly in his dealings with Isra'el. What other god has ever lifted a nation out of slavery and into freedom as ADONAI redeemed Isra'el from Egypt? That act alone shows him to be a holy-other God, calling a nation to be a holy-other people: "You will be...a nation set apart" (Exod. 19:6). It is based on that act alone that the holy God has the right to call the nation to holiness: "Be holy, for I am holy" (Lev. 11:44). Yesha'yahu records God's grief over Isra'el in these words:

> Oh, sinful nation,
> a people weighed down by iniquity,
> descendants of evildoers,
> immoral children!
> They have abandoned ADONAI
> spurned the Holy One of Isra'el,
> turned their backs on him! (Isa. 1:4)

The God of Isra'el Only?

The ancient world saw 'gods' as local deities, each to be respected in their own place. Indeed, the modern world has returned to this philosophy, with its emphasis on the equal value of every belief system. ADONAI, however, is entirely different. Yes, he is Isra'el's God, but he is also the 'one' God. There is no other. Sha'ul explores this connection in his letter to the Romans: "Is God the God of the Jews only? Isn't he also the God of the Gentiles? Yes, he is indeed the God of the Gentiles; because, as you will admit, God is one" (Rom. 3:29–30). Nanos points out that the assertion of God's particularism in relation to Isra'el was also used by Sha'ul. He was showing that God's universalism was embedded in the monotheistic faith of Isra'el. The one God of Isra'el was also the one God of the nations (Nanos, 181).

Yeshua

For Yeshua, the "uniqueness" of Isra'el was taken for granted. He certainly would identify with the words of the prayer *Ahavat Olam* (Everlasting Love): "You have loved Isra'el, your people, with everlasting love…. Blessed are you, Lord, who loves Isra'el, your people."

Yeshua came first to "his own." He loved his own and grieved over his own. However, it seems that grief was not primarily for her political situation, but for her estrangement from God: "Yerushalayim! Yerushalayim! You kill the prophets! You stone those who are sent to you! How often I wanted to gather your children, just as a hen gathers her chickens under her wings, but you refused!" (Matt. 23:37).

The peripheral vision was all-important to Yeshua. Isra'el was his immediate concern, but the world was always in his view. Anybody involved with him was to "go and make people from all nations into *talmidim*" (Matt. 28:19). This was in keeping with God's promise to Avraham (Abraham): "By your descendants all the nations of the earth will be blessed" (Gen. 22:18). Choice is always for a purpose, a wider purpose, God's purpose.

Sha'ul never lost his heart for his own people, always going to the synagogues first. He too yearned over Isra'el: "My heart's deepest desire and my prayer to God for Isra'el is for their salvation" (Rom. 10:1). He too saw the wider picture; Isra'el's salvation would be "life from the dead" for the world (Rom. 11:15).

Strength in Weakness

Ya'akov emerged from Peniel as Isra'el—marked by physical weakness. Sha'ul too had to learn this lesson. Something troubled him that he seemed to see as a hindrance to his ministry. He begged the

Lord, persistently, to relieve him of this thing. "Enough already," said the Lord! "My grace is enough for you, for my power is brought to perfection in weakness" (2 Cor. 12:9). Sha'ul was able to take this truth to heart, and pass it on to newer believers. We are just like poor quality pots containing treasure, he said. Nobody will praise the pots—all will see our weakness and realize that the power we have comes from God, not ourselves (2 Cor. 4:7).

For Thought

It is no easy matter to be Isra'el. Isra'el is a person, a people, reduced in strength and yet empowered by an encounter with God. Isra'el is a person, a people, who have faced the truth about themselves and about God. Isra'el is a person, a people, called to be different, never to be anonymous in the crowd, head always above the parapet. Isra'el is a person, a people, required by God and expected by the world to live to higher standards of ethics and integrity. Isra'el is a person, a people, called to impact the world for good and for truth. Who would choose to be Isra'el?

Believers in Yeshua lay claim to having been adopted into Isra'el. Sha'ul uses a horticultural image. We have been grafted onto the rootstock that is Isra'el (Rom. 11:17). That being the case, we must be prepared to take on board much more than the blessings and the promises. Being part of Isra'el is to be a person who has had an encounter with God on his terms, and been changed by that encounter. It is to be a person whose strength has become weakness and whose weakness has become strength. Worldly success no longer will have value. Worldly failure will no longer hold shame. To be part of Isra'el is to be a new man, a new woman. It is to identify with the pain, as well as the privilege, of Isra'el.

These believers have a calling echoing that of Isra'el. Sha'ul expressed it like this: "To know him [Yeshua], that is, to know the power of his resurrection and the fellowship of his sufferings as I am being conformed to his death, so that somehow I might arrive at being resurrected from the dead" (Phil. 3:10). That, said Sha'ul, was "God's upward calling in the Messiah Yeshua" (v.14). Being the called of the Lord is never going to be easy or comfortable—or even necessarily successful. It requires a spirit of brokenness, an admission of weakness, a total acknowledgment of God, and a confidence in the future. The path to resurrection will lead through suffering. Conversely, the path of the Cross leads to resurrection and glory.

To be Isra'el is to be a princely people—a people with a future and a hope. However, this future is not based on our own achievements. We have simply heard his call and responded to his love. From now on we are his people and he is our God.

The Christian Church has always laid great stress on individual salvation. Yeshua did indeed address individuals. He came so that *whosoever* trusted in him would have life. The community of believers is made up of individuals who are committed disciples of the Messiah-Savior. However, those individuals do form a community. Isra'el is community. I suggest that gentile believers are not always good at community, at least in the western world. That is one of the reasons why Messianic Jews often do not feel comfortable in gentile churches. They miss the warmth. If we claim to be part of Isra'el we need to unbend a little, share ourselves, and be open to one another.

A Prayer

> Lord, I live in a culture where weakness is despised and humility misunderstood; where success is sought after above all else. I have to confess to you that my fellow believers and I are deeply contaminated by this culture. I want to lay at your feet my desire to achieve, to succeed, and to be seen to succeed. Let me see myself as *you* want me to be, not as *I* want to be. Bring me to the place where I no longer want to hide my inner self from my fellow believers; where I truly yearn for nothing more than to be identified with my Messiah—in his suffering, his Cross, and his death. I know that this is true achievement, true success, and true resurrection life.
>
> Blessed are you, O Lord our God, King of the universe, who does not despise a humble and contrite heart.

CHAPTER 3

The Lord Our God

יהוה אֱלֹהֵינוּ

ADONAI Eloheynu

"When God gave the Law, no bird sang or flew, no ox bellowed, the angels did not fly, the Seraphim ceased from saying, 'Holy, holy,' the sea was calm, no creature spoke; the world was silent and still, and the divine voice said: 'I am the Lord thy God....'" (Montefiore, 2)

A Person, Not a "Force"

The Ten Words (Commandments) begin with the statement: "I am ADONAI your God" (Exod. 20:2). Jewish people never write or speak the Ineffable Name (YHVH). The customary rendering is "ADONAI." In English Bibles it appears as "the LORD." YHVH is the One who is, who was, and who is to come. This is the God who made himself known to Isra'el through Moshe (Exod. 3:13–15). Moshe wanted to know his name, and the answer was "Ehyeh Asher Ehyeh" (I am/ will be what I am/will be).

This God is life and the source of life. So it is that Maimonides' first principle states:

> I firmly believe that the Creator, blessed be his name, is both Creator and Ruler of all created beings, and that he alone is the active cause of all things, whether past, present, or future.

For Jewish people, the first precept is to believe in the existence of God. This is the basis and foundation of everything that follows. Furthermore, this God is no impersonal force, an 'It.' He is the one who introduces himself as "Anokhi" (I) as he pronounces these Ten Words. He is the source not only of life. He is the fountainhead of everything that goes to make up humanity, everything that makes each of us what we are.

The Two Names

Two names seem to be describing quite different facets of the character of God. *Elohim* is God. YHVH is ADONAI, the LORD. There is an unwillingness to speak this name, even as ADONAI. The custom is to use another title, usually *HaShem* (the name), as a euphemism.

Elohim is the Creator and Master of all Creation. He is the God of universal power. He is transcendent, even impersonal. His goodness is that of perfect orderliness. He represents the *middat-ha-din* (the attribute of divine judgment). Elohim inspires awe. Before him, we are small and insignificant.

Hashem (ADONAI) is the Lord of history, who sometimes intervenes in human affairs. His goodness is moral, relating to people. He represents *middat-ha-rahamim* (the attribute of divine mercy). He is immanent, involved with the people he created, and even seeks relationship with them. He gives and desires love. *Hashem* it is who has a special relationship with the Children of Isra'el.

It is important to realize that we are speaking of one God only. The two attributes are not contradictory. As God said through the prophet Yesha'yahu: "I form light, I create darkness; I make well-being, I create woe; I, ADONAI, do all these things" (Isa. 45:7). There is only one God, but his nature is so complex that finite people need different words to describe him. All attributes of the one God are good.

The four letters, YHVH, are known as the Tetragrammaton. The pronunciation of this is unknown. It is always pronounced as "ADONAI." The word "*HaShem*" literally means "the name," and is the form usually spoken, except in the liturgy. This custom has developed as a way of showing respect to the Almighty. It also guards against profane use of his name. It is the name associated with God's special relationship with Isra'el, dating back to their deliverance from Egypt and the giving of Torah on Sinai. We could perhaps call *HaShem* God's "Jewish name." It is the name, which we associate with God's manifestation to Moshe on Sinai: YHVH "is God, merciful and compassionate, slow to anger, rich in grace and truth...." (Exod. 34:6).

Names are more than just labels in Hebrew culture. They actually represent the person. That is why we choose names with great care. They say something about the child's identity. They mirror the parents' hopes and ambitions for that child. Yesha'yahu gave us a long list of names for the coming Messiah, which describe a whole range of his activities and ministry. His name would be *Immanu El*, because that means "God with us" (Isa. 7:14). His name would be "Wonder of a Counselor, Mighty God, Father of Eternity, Prince of Peace" (Isa. 9:7(6)). All these titles reveal something of the ministry of the coming Messiah. He would be wise; he would bring peace; he would be eternal and divine.

"*ADONAI*" (LORD) is an acceptable rendering of this name, because it describes a relationship. The nation delivered from slavery in Egypt is now free. However, that freedom is in the context of a master-servant relationship with the God who brought about their deliverance. Every time we say the Sh'ma we can remember that we are free people. The only *adon* (lord, master) we have is ADONAI *Eloheynu* (the LORD our God). He it is who redeemed us from slavery, and set us free to serve him as Lord and Master.

Eloheynu (Our God)

The words "*our God*" imply a very special relationship. God has chosen to place his name upon Isra'el. Remember the words concerning the Aaronic Blessing:

Y'varekh'kha ADONAI *v'yishmerekha.*
[May ADONAI bless you and keep you.]

Ya'er ADONAI *panav eleikha vichunekha.*
[May ADONAI make his face shine on you and show you his favor.]

Yissa ADONAI *panav eleikha v'yasem l'kha shalom.*
[May ADONAI lift up his face toward you and give you peace.]

"In this way they are to put my name on the people of Isra'el, so that I will bless them" (Num. 6:24–27). To have God's name put upon us is a tremendous privilege. He publicly owns us as his children. It is as if he were like those of us who are parents, when we introduce one of our children to someone special. You stand tall before this person, your arm round your child's shoulders, and say proudly, "This is my son, my daughter." I remember an occasion when I was publicly honored, and my father was in the hall. I saw his face. He was so proud. It was one of the best experiences of my life, realizing that my father was proud of me. God is not ashamed to acknowledge Isra'el.

The great second century rabbi Akiba taught that all people are created and loved by God. However, Isra'el has a special place in God's heart: "Beloved are Isra'el, in that they are called sons of God...to make known to Isra'el this high calling was a further mark of love" (*Av.* 3:18). The prayer, "*Mi Khamokha*" (Who is like you), recalls Isra'el's song of praise after crossing the Sea of Reeds. What is it that made Isra'el see God as unique at this time? It was what he had done for *them*: "In your love, you led the people you redeemed; in your strength, you guided them to your holy abode" (Exod. 15:13). God also sees this historic experience as crucial. How many times he speaks to them saying, "I am the Lord your God, who brought you out of the land of Egypt, out of the house of bondage."

All this means that Isra'el owes an undivided loyalty to the God who is hers. Some would even translate the words of the Sh'ma in such a way as to reinforce this. Instead of the usual "the LORD our God", they say, "The LORD *is* our God." If we are to be his people then he must be our God. This is the eternal covenant relationship. It has its origins in history, it exists today, and it will persist into the future. "I will be their God, and they will be my people." That relationship is fundamental to everything that Isra'el is. A relationship carries awesome responsibilities. Isra'el bears God's name. Isra'el represents God among the nations.

Whether a Jewish person recites the Sh'ma alone or in the congregation he still uses the plural: "the LORD *our* God." This is a relationship with a nation, not with a disparate group of individuals. In the prayer "*Modim*" (Thanksgivings) we say: "We give thanks unto You, for You are the Lord *our* God and the God of *our* fathers for ever and ever; You are the Rock of *our* lives, *our* saving shield through every generation." In the Days of Awe, leading up to *Yom Kippur* (the Day of Atonement), Jewish people make their individual preparations, healing relationships, setting things right. However, on Yom Kippur itself, the prayers of confession are communal. "For the sin wherein we have sinned...O God of forgiveness, forgive us, pardon us, grant us atonement." It is hardly possible to be a Jewish person apart from the community of Isra'el.

Nevertheless, we should each seek after personal righteousness. "*ELOHIM ADONAI* is *my* strength" (Hab. 3:19, italics mine). The rabbis see it to be important for each individual to acknowledge God's lordship. "You may have recognized the lofty vocation of Israel," said Hirsch, "without feeling *yourself* to be in every fiber a son or daughter of Israel. So long as this is so, your knowledge is barren" (Hirsch, 3). The personal responsibilities of this relationship can be summed up in these words, which Hirsch describes as "the threshold of Jewish life":

> 'I the Lord am thy God' —I am your Creator, your Lawgiver, your Judge; the Director of your thoughts, your feelings, your words and your actions. Every one of your internal and external possessions has come to you from My hand; every breath of your life has been apportioned to you by Me. Look upon yourself and all that is yours as My property, and devote yourself wholly to Me, with every fraction of your property, every moment of your time; with mind, feeling, bodily strength and means, with words and action. Be the instrument, the agent of My will with all that has accrued or will accrue to you; and so join freely the choir of creation as My creature, My servant, as a man and an Israelite. (Hirsch, 4)

The Other Nations?

The words "our God" suggest special responsibility, special destiny, not exclusivity. Rashi, the great eleventh century French biblical and talmudic commentator, explained that the meaning is: The Lord is now our God and not yet the God of the other nations, though he will be one day when the promise of Tz'fanyah (Zephaniah) 3:9 is realized (Rashi, *Deuteronomy* 37). That promise reads, "Then I will change the peoples, so that they will have pure lips, to call on the name of *ADONAI*, all of them, and serve him with one accord."

There is never any suggestion that God has no concern for the other nations, the foreign peoples. There is a tradition that God rebuked the angels in heaven when they rejoiced over the drowning of the Egyptians in the Sea of Reeds. He exclaimed: "My creatures die in the sea, and you sing songs!" That is why at the Passover *seder* (order of service) we remove a drop of wine from our cups for every plague inflicted on the Egyptians.

There is a lovely word in the Talmud concerning all mankind: "The Holy One, blessed be He, fashioned every man in the image of the first man, yet not one of them resembles his fellow. Therefore every single person must say, 'The world was created for my sake'" (*San.* 37a).

God So Loved the World

Yeshua carried this last thought much further. For the world's sake God sent his Son, so that the world might be saved. Moreover, each one of us, Jew and Gentile, can say, "For *my* sake was God's only Son given" (John 3:16–17). Through Yeshua it is possible for both Jew and Gentile to say "*my* God" as well as "*our* God." Through the covenant blood (Matt. 26:28) all can claim that covenant relationship in which he is our God and we are his people. Yeshua taught his *talmidim* to pray, "Our Father...." There comes a time, though, in every life, when each of us has to confess with Thomas, "My Lord and my God" (John 20:28).

For Thought

It is easy to get the balance wrong here. Some have no sense of community at all, only a realization that "*I* have been born again; *I* am saved." I may see no value in attending a place of worship; at best I may hop from congregation to congregation, always receiving, never giving; always tasting, never committing. The fact is that God is interested in community. He called Isra'el as a community. Yeshua talked of his plan to build *his* community—the messianic community (Matt. 16:18). Sha'ul spent his life not only bringing individuals to belief and salvation, but also establishing communities of believers. He saw the messianic community as a body in which different parts and limbs have different functions, but all are necessary to the whole (Rom. 12:4–5). Another picture is that of a building, whose various parts need to fit together so that the whole structure will be sound (Eph. 2: 21).

Some go to the opposite extreme, setting so much store on membership of the nation, the community, that they may ignore individual responsibility. They may even lose sight of the value of themselves and others as individuals. Others may think little of me; I may take a poor view of myself. The fact is that Almighty God set such a high value on me that he gave his only Son to save me from death into life. That means I am worth a very great deal. It also means that I owe a very great debt. God is now not only "my God"; he is also "my Lord." We are in a master-servant relationship. He is mine and I am his.

> As a servant looks to the hand of his master,
> or a slave-girl to the hand of her mistress,
> so our eyes turn to ADONAI our God,
> until he has mercy on us. (Ps. 123:2)

A Prayer

Lord, thank you for setting such a high value on me. I do not feel I am worth that much, but you do, or you would not have paid such a price. You are my God and I am your child. How blessed I am! Please help me to accept my worth. I know too that I need to give myself to the community to which you call me. Please make clear to me where I am to be. I cannot walk alone, neither do you want me to wander from congregation to congregation. I need to be in a community, to worship and serve in that community, and join with that community in proclaiming: "The Lord is *our* God."

> We give thanks to our God, our Sovereign, our
>   Redeemer.
> Praised be our God, our Sovereign, our Redeemer.
> You are our God, our Sovereign, our Redeemer.
>   (*Eyn Keloheynu. Siddur lev Chadash*, 528)

Blessed are you, O Lord our God, King of the universe, who chose us in love to be his own people.

CHAPTER 4

The Lord Is One

יְהוָֹה אֶחָד

ADONAI *Echad*

"I firmly believe that the Creator, blessed be his name, is One; that there is no oneness like his, in any way, and that he alone was, is, and will be our God" (Maimonides' second principle).

> Thou art One, and in the mystery of Thy Oneness the wise of heart are astonished, for they know not what it is. Thou art One, and Thy Oneness neither diminishes nor increases, neither lacks nor exceeds. Thou art One, but not as the one that is counted or owned, for number and chance cannot reach Thee, nor attribute, nor form. Thou art One, but my mind is too feeble to set Thee a law or a limit, and therefore I say: "I will take heed to my ways, that I sin not with my tongue." Thou art One, and Thou art exalted above abasement and falling—not like a man, who falls when he is alone. (Solomon Ibn Gabirol (c. 1021-1058), *The Kingly Crown*. Plaut 1373)

"God is a unity is affirmed from one's earliest years until death." That is how my late husband, Eric Lipson, expressed it.

Yihud HaShem—the unity of God

Belief in the unity of God is the basic tenet of Judaism—its foundation stone. Monotheism has been Jewry's great gift to the world. Lamm goes as far as to say: "These two words—*Hashem ehad*, 'the Lord is One' —constitute probably the most significant and revolutionary phrase in the entire lexicon of Jewish thought" (Lamm, 31).

27

The idea of the oneness of God is awesome. On Sinai, according to tradition, the whole world held silence so that every creature might realize that there is no God but ADONAI. To reinforce this awesomeness, the practice developed of stressing and drawing out the word *Echad* (One) in the recitation of the Sh'ma. The origin of this practice may be the story of the great Rabbi Akiba. He died under torture with this word on his lips, and the *Bat Kol* (Voice of God) announced: "Happy art thou, Akiba, that thy soul has departed with the word ehad!" (*Ber.* 61b).

Isra'el has stood for *Yihud HaShem* since the time of the Patriarchs. There are several legends about Avraham that credit him with being the first to take a stand against the futile worship of the many gods of those days. One of them tells how when he was three years old he went out one night and saw the stars. "Surely these must be God, and I will worship them," he thought. Then morning came, the stars seemed to be no longer there, and he concluded that they could not be God. Then the sun came out, and he said, "This must be God." The sun set and the moon arose and he said, "Perhaps this is God." Then the angel Gabriel came down and told him that God is the One who created the stars, the sun, the moon, and all that exists. Then Abraham bowed down and prayed to the Lord, the creator of heaven and earth.

This belief in only one God was set in stone at Sinai: "You are to have no other gods before me" (Exod. 20:3). It is likely that the practice of constantly reciting these words goes back to the time of the Exile in Babylon. It may be that in those dark, demoralized days the people began to lose faith in their Lord, and the religious leaders ordained this practice to counteract a slide into idolatry. Now, they are a watchword, a constant reminder throughout life that there is only one God. This is the God we are to love. He stands alone. He is not one among many gods. He is not even the greatest among many gods. He is the only true God.

Judaism sees the doctrine of the unity of God as distinguishing it from all other religions. It is the particular mark of the Jewish people, and has been since ancient times when polytheism was the norm. It is the creed, which Jewish people state constantly and live by. It is a recurring theme in Jewish literature. It is the belief for which many have sacrificed their lives.

Incomparable—Unique

Echad can also mean 'unique'—totally different in quality. The story of *Hanukkah* (the Feast of Dedication) tells of another dark period in Isra'el's history. The tyrant, Antiochus IV Epiphanes, had ordered the elimination of every religious practice, everything that defined Jewish people as worshippers of the one God. Eventually the Maccabees, the sons of Mattathias the priest, stirred up the people to revolt. Their rallying cry was, "Who is like unto Thee, O Lord, among the gods?" This echoed the song of triumph after the Isra'elites had crossed the Sea of Reeds:

> Who is like you, ADONAI, among the mighty?
> Who is like you, sublime in holiness,
> awesome in praises, working wonders? (Exod. 15:11)

These words have become a refrain in the Jewish liturgy. The synagogue prayer that follows the Sh'ma, *Mi Khamokha*, begins like this:

> Who is like You, Eternal One, among the gods the people worship? *Siddur lev Chadash* 16.

One of the best-known songs chanted in synagogue is *Eyn Keloheynu*:

> *Eyn keloheynu, eyn kadoneynu,*
> [There is none like our God, there is none like our Lord,]
>
> *eyn k'malkheynu, eyn k'moshieynu,*
> [There is none like our King, there is none like our Redeemer.]

Rabbi Akiba was once asked the meaning of the oneness of God. His reply veered towards a qualitative interpretation, rather than a purely quantitative one. He saw God as utterly unique in the whole universe. As the Creator of everything, every creature, and every person, he knows everything about them all. Nothing is a mystery to him.

Unchanging

God's oneness also means absolute consistency. He may act in different ways at different times; he may express himself in different ways in different situations, but in his essential nature he is always the same. The rabbis insist that we may discern different attributes in his character, but it is always the same God, all of him. He acts in many different ways, and reveals different facets of himself. Yet he remains constant, unchanging, always true to himself.

The Prime Cause

Maimonides' first principle places God unequivocally as the sole active cause of all things, past, present, and future. This means that Creation too has a unity. The Creator has set in place the laws of nature which man, with all his abilities, is powerless to rival or to change.

Spinoza, the seventeenth century Dutch thinker, saw that a sole Creator must necessarily be superior to all else. This doctrine was, in his eyes, essential to a right view of God, and a right attitude in worship. If we are to relate rightly to God, this must be our starting point. We cannot truly love him if we are uncertain about his worth (Plaut, 1373. Citing Spinoza. *Theologico-Political Treatise* 14).

No Other To Be Worshipped

If God is *the* only God, then it follows that he must be *our* only God, *my* only God. The second Word from Sinai commands: "You are to have no other gods before me [literally, before my face]" (Exod. 20:3). This does not mean that we must have no other gods taking priority before him, above him, in status. No. We are to have no other gods at all. The *Alenu*, a prayer said at the close of most synagogue services, includes these words:

> He is our God; there is no other. He is our King, truly, there is none beside Him, just as it is written in his Torah: "You shall know this day, and keep it in your heart, that the Lord, He is God in heaven above and on the earth beneath. There is none else." (Budoff, 28)

Maimonides affirmed this too in his fourth principle: "I firmly believe that the Creator, blessed be his name, alone is worthy of being worshipped, and that no other being is worthy of our worship." The logical corollary of God's uniqueness is that he alone is to be worshipped.

God is alone. The Talmud has a comment on God's oneness. "The Holy One, blessed be He, said to Israel, 'My children, everything that I created in the universe is in pairs—heaven and earth, the sun and moon, Adam and Eve, this world and the world to come; but I am one and alone in the universe'" (*Deut. R.* 2:31).

Omnipresent

If there is only one God, he must necessarily be eternal and omnipresent. Otherwise his activity would be limited to one place and one time period. He would, indeed, not be God at all. So another expression of the belief in God's oneness is to say that he fills all of space. There is nowhere where God is not. The *Alenu* prayer quotes Deuteronomy:

> Know today, and establish it in your heart, that ADONAI is God in heaven above and on earth below—there is no other. (Deut. 4:39)

This has massive implications. It means that the planet is not out of control. God sees all and is never taken unawares. It means too that individuals cannot escape him forever. David made a discovery that can be either frightening or supremely comforting:

> Where can I go to escape your Spirit?
> Where can I flee from your presence?
> If I climb up to heaven, you are there;
> if I lie down in Sh'ol, you are there.
> If I fly away with the wings of the dawn
> and land beyond the sea,
> even there your hand would lead me,
> your right hand would hold me fast. (Ps. 139:7–10)

The Human Implications

Hertz points out that belief in the unity of God leads logically to belief in the unity of the whole human race. It follows, therefore, that worshipping and praying to the One God must involve dedicating ourselves to bringing peace among all people (Hertz, *Authorised Daily Prayer Book with Commentary* 265).

This can be taken even further. We need to be unified individuals, integrated, balanced, whole. Wholeness is implied in the greeting we give one another—*Shalom*. Our religious life should not be isolated from the rest of life. Neither should it cause us to isolate ourselves from other people. We are to be single-hearted, as God is. "You must comprehend your life with all its diversity as proceeding from this One and you must direct it towards this One, in order that your life may be a unity just as your God is One" (Hirsch, 6).

Isra'el's Duty

The proclamation of the oneness of God symbolizes the mission of Isra'el to the world:

> With the Law of God folded in his arms and its words engraved upon his heart, he [the Jew] has gone up and down the earth proclaiming his belief in the One Supreme Being—a Being whose spirit fills all time and all space, a Being never embodied, but made manifest to man in the glory of the creation and in his all-wise behests, which teach mercy, love, and justice. (Hermann Adler, *The Mission of Israel*. From Hertz, *A Book of Jewish Thoughts* 24)

The Trinity

Compared with Judaism's strong assertion of God's oneness, Christianity appears to Jewish eyes to be polytheism; that is the worship of more than one god. The doctrine of the Trinity is incomprehensible to those who have been reared from the cradle on *Yihud HaShem*. To them it is inconceivable that the Messiah should be a divine figure. He, when he comes, will be a man—a man anointed by God, a man above other men—but still a man.

Yeshua did, however, claim to be more than just human. He claimed oneness with the Father (John 10:30). He said that those who had seen him had seen the Father (John 14:9). My husband, an Orthodox Jew who had to face this difficulty before committing himself to Yeshua as Messiah, came to this conclusion: "Unity, however, is not singularity. Genesis tells us that evening and morning together are one day, and that two persons, Adam and Eve, became one flesh. *Eloheynu, HaShem echad*—our God (a plural word in Hebrew), the Lord is one, refers to the one God who is a unity."

Sha'ul

Sha'ul found it necessary to confront the belief that Gentiles must convert to Judaism in order to become full-fledged members of the Messianic community. In the letter to the Romans he based his position upon the oneness of God. If there is only one God, he argued, then he must be the God of the Gentiles also. To suggest otherwise is to conclude that there is one God for Jews and another for Gentiles: "Is God the God of the Jews only? Isn't he also the God of the Gentiles? Yes, he is indeed the God of the Gentiles; because, as you will admit, God is one. Therefore, he will consider righteous the circumcised on the ground of trusting and the uncircumcised through that same trusting" (Rom. 3:29–30). Nanos puts it like this: "The God who demonstrated his faithfulness to Israel is the one and only God. He must also be the God of the Gentiles who call on the One God through faith in Christ Jesus. To assert otherwise, Paul argued, would be to compromise God's oneness" (Nanos 182).

For Thought

ADONAI claims to be the only God, and there is no other. Yeshua identified with *HaShem*, and claimed to be the only way to the only God: "I AM the Way—and the Truth and the Life; no one comes to the Father except through me. Because you have known me, you will also know my Father; from now on, you do know him—in fact, you have seen him" (John 14:6–7). To hold this view is not politically correct. It will win us no popularity. We shall meet intense pressure to compromise on the question of who and what Yeshua is.

This question is particularly acute for Messianic Jews. It always has been. That is why the letter to Messianic Jews (Hebrews) opens with these words:

> In days gone by, God spoke in many and varied ways to the Fathers through the prophets. But now, in the *acharit hayamim* [last days], he has spoken to us through his Son, to whom he has given ownership of everything and through whom he created the universe. This Son is the radiance of the *Sh'khinah*, the very expression of God's essence. (Heb. 1:1–3)

Whom shall we believe? Whom shall we choose? Whom shall we serve?

> He is One, and there is no second
> to compare Him or to place next to Him.
> He has no beginning and no end;
> Power and dominion are his.
>
> He is my living God who saves,
> My Rock when troubles and sorrows are mine;
> My Banner and my strong refuge,
> My bounteous portion whenever I call.
>
> I give my soul into his care,
> For He is near when I sleep and when I wake.
> With my soul, my body too;
> God is with me, I shall not be afraid. (*Adon Olam*. Budoff, 94)

A Prayer

Lord God, the God of my fathers, I will stand firm and be true to you. I will be among the number who sing "the song of Moshe, the servant of God, and the song of the Lamb":

> Great and wonderful are the things you have done,
> ADONAI, God of heaven's armies!
> Just and true are your ways,
> king of the nations!
> ADONAI, who will not fear and glorify your name?
> because you alone are holy.
> All nations will come and worship before you....
> (Rev. 15:3–4)

Blessed are you, Father in heaven, Savior Yeshua, *Ruakh HaKodesh* (Holy Spirit); the One true God.

CHAPTER 5

Blessed Be His Glorious Name

בָּרוּךְ שֵׁם כָּבוֹד

Barukh Shem Kavod

There is an inserted sentence added after the first six words of the Sh'ma: "Blessed be his glorious name whose kingdom is forever and ever." These words are not biblical, and their origin is uncertain. One legend attributes them to the patriarch Ya'akov, speaking to his sons from his deathbed (Gen. 49). The Talmud tells us he wanted reassurance that there was no unfaithfulness among his sons. He was mindful of Avraham's and Yitz'chak's experiences with their sons Yishma'el and Esav, who both failed to continue in their fathers' godly tradition. Would there be unfaithfulness among the sons of Isra'el also? Would they continue to worship the One God after his death? It seems they responded, together: "Hear O Isra'el, the Lord our God, the Lord is One; just as there is only One in thy heart, so is there in our heart only One." Ya'akov—much relieved—then exclaimed, "Blessed be the name of his glorious Kingdom for ever and ever" (*Pes.* 56a).

Another story is that when Moshe went up the mountain to God, he heard the worshipping angels saying these words to God. He then brought them down to the Isra'elites in the camp.

The words developed as a response. It seems that in Temple times, the people spoke them, as they prostrated themselves, on hearing the *Kohen HaGadol* (High Priest) say the Ineffable Name—YHVH. They then became the customary response to the first verse of the Sh'ma (*Taanit* 16b), and this practice was later transferred to the synagogue. We speak them as a doxology, instead of saying "Amen." In saying these words we are affirming our agreement with the declaration that has gone before.

37

Sotto Voce

The custom is to recite this sentence quietly, almost under the breath. Why? There are various explanations. Here is an ancient one: "The matter is like as if a man stole a jewel from the King's palace, and gave it to his wife, and said to her, 'Do not deck yourself with it publicly, but only within the house'" (Montefiore and Loewe, 3). A modern comment by Donin refers back to the Ya'akov tradition. The patriarch was dying, and he spoke these words in weakness. Jewish people today speak them quietly to symbolize that weakness. The Talmud has another, more down-to-earth explanation: it tells us that we should say them in this way to indicate that it is not a part of the biblical text (*Pes.* 56a).

On *Yom Kippur*, however, one says the words aloud. This is perhaps to demonstrate robustly that we are a forgiven people, free of guilt. As such we can speak the words as boldly as the angels who minister in the presence of God (Montefiore, 3).

Why These Words?

The suggestion is that the first verse of the Sh'ma demands a response. We have stated that God is utterly "other," unique. We need to respond, here—now, to what he is. We live in a real world, not an abstract one. After the sublime first sentence we come down to earth, back to our human world, with its human limitations, bringing the sublime into that world. We declare our intention of being worthy to serve God

In Temple times, *Barukh Shem Kavod* (Blessed be his Glorious Name) was the response of the people to hearing the High Priest pronounce the Ineffable Name on *Yom Kippur*. God's name is his person, his character, who he is. So we bless the Creator-God, the God who is, was, and will be; the God who graciously interacts with us, meeting our needs, forgiving our sins.

Alternative Translations

There are several ways of translating these words. Budoff's perhaps conforms most closely to the accepted renderings of Nehemiah 9:5

and Psalm 72:19: "Blessed is his glorious name, whose kingdom is for ever and ever." Here are some other renderings:

> Blessed be his name, whose glorious kingdom is forever and ever (Singer, 8).
> Blessed is the name of his glorious majesty forever and ever (Donin, 146).
> Blessed be the name of his glorious kingdom for ever and ever (Lamm, 69).

The Importance of the Name

Hebrew thought closely associates the name with the person. The name can reveal the character. A rose by another name does *not* smell as sweet! The third prayer in the *Amidah* includes these words: "Thou art holy, and thy name is holy." The holiness of the name of God reflects God's essential holiness.

The concepts of *Kiddush HaShem* (sanctification of the name) and *Chillul HaShem* (profanation of the name) have arisen because of this identification of the name with the Person. To sanctify the name of God is to honor God himself. To profane his name is to blaspheme against God himself.

Judaism is always mindful of the need to sanctify God's name. We can do this in three ways: by an act of martyrdom, by a high standard of moral conduct, or by proclaiming God's holiness in public prayer. Lamm suggests that this third *mitzvah* is performed as a dialogue, the congregation responding to a statement by the reader. This means that every member of the congregation participates personally in the proclamation. Since the second sentence was a response to the mention of the divine name, it fits into this third category of *Kiddush HaShem* (Lamm, 69–70).

We can learn about other aspects of God's character by looking at his names—and there many such names. Here are some of them:

> *El Shaddai* (the Almighty)
> *Elohim* (God)
> ADONAI *Tzva'ot* (the Lord of hosts)
> *HaMakom* (the Place)

HaKadosh (the Holy One)
Av HaRakhamim (Father of mercies)
HaVayah (the One who is)
Av she baShamayim (Father in heaven)

The Tetragrammaton

The most sacred name of God is known as the Tetragrammaton—literally "4 letters"—יהוה (*YHVH*). It is the "I AM" name, dating back to the words of God to Moshe, at his commissioning. Asked to identify himself, his reply was, "*Ehyeh Asher Ehyeh*" (I am/will be what I am/will be)." He then added, "Here is what to say to the people of Isra'el: '*Ehyeh* (I Am/Will Be) has sent me to you'" (Exod. 3:14). Known in Judaism as "the Ineffable Name," *YHVH* is regarded as so holy that it is neither written nor spoken. In its place we find "*ADONAI*" (the LORD).

The refusal to write or speak the name is really the culmination of belief in God's holiness, and the fear of inadvertently committing *Chillul HaShem*. In ancient times there seems to have been no such prohibition. Cohen points out that "the addition of Yah or Yahu to personal names, which persisted among the Jews even after the Babylonian exile, is an indication that there was no prohibition against the employment of the four-lettered name" (Cohen, 25). By the early rabbinical period, though, even while the Temple was still standing, the name was spoken in Temple services but not elsewhere. It was not until some time in the last years before the Temple was destroyed in C.E.70 that its pronunciation was forbidden. However, the earliest evidence of the dread of using this name is in the Septuagint, the Greek translation of the Hebrew Scriptures, compiled around the third century B.C.E., where it is rendered as "Kurios" (Lord). Josephus, writing in the second century C.E., said that it was not lawful for him to "say any more" about God's holy name (*Antiquities* 2.12,§4). The Talmud, speaking of the world to come, says, "The future world is not like this world. Here the name of God is written vuvh [*YHVH*] and read hbst [*ADONAI*]; there it is also read vuvh" (*Pes.* 50a). Today, the true pronunciation of the Ineffable Name is not known.

Sometimes the title *Shem HaMeforash* is used; this is an ancient way of saying "that name of God which is apart from all his other names" (*Sot.* 38a). It is quite common for Jewish writers to satisfy the prohibition by leaving out the central letter in "God." Thus, "G-d." Usually the term employed is "*HaShem*" (literally "the name").

The Holiness of God

Holiness implies apartness as well as perfection. God is not only pure; he is all together different, other. The Talmud comments that in Joshua's words, "He is a holy God" (Josh. 24:19), the word "holy" is plural. This means, "He is holy with all kinds of holiness." In other words, he is the perfection of holiness (*Ber.* 13a). God's holiness is absolute and total; it is beyond anything attainable by people.

This apartness means that God is unapproachable. The people could not approach the mountain at Sinai; neither could they look at Moses' face when the glory was shining on him. Fire is a good imageglorious, but dangerous. Moses had to tread carefully and reverently at the burning bush. Yesha'yahu was terrified at the sight of the glory, because he knew he was unworthy to look upon it; so God symbolically cleansed him with fire. This experience made such an impression on him that he consistently thereafter referred to God as "the Holy One of Isra'el."

There is the belief that we must guard God's holiness from any kind of profanation. Things that are used for worship are not to be used in ordinary ways. The people set apart for God—Isra'el—is to guard her holiness: "You are a people set apart as holy for ADONAI your God" (Deut. 7:6). The Jewish Encyclopedia puts it like this: "The entire system of the Jewish law has the hallowing of life as its aim, to be reached through good works, through observance of the Sabbath and holy days, and through the sanctification of God's name" (Vol. 6. 441., Holiness).

Blessing the Name

Sometimes Jewish people use the term, "The Holy One, blessed be he," when speaking of God. Frequently, the words are *Barukh haShem* (Blessed be the Name) or *Barukh hu uvarukh Shemo* (Blessed be he and blessed be his Name). When we bless the name, as in the inserted sentence of the Sh'ma, we are recognizing the holiness and glory of the Almighty himself, and acknowledging his apartness.

There is None Like Him

Two prayers commonly spoken in the liturgy emphasize the apartness, the uniqueness, of God. They are *Mi Khamokha* (Who is like you?) and *Eyn Keloheynu* (There is none like our God—our Lord—our King—our Deliverer). Both these prayers associate God's innate holiness and glory with his redemptive action in delivering Isra'el from Egypt.

Yeshua

It is not surprising that God was concerned about the name he would give to his incarnate Son, the Messiah. What was to be his work? He was to save his people from their sins. What, then, should be his name? Why, "Salvation" of course. Yeshua means "YHVH saves." "You are to name him Yeshua, because he will save his people from their sins" (Matt. 1:21).

Yochanan records an interesting event in the life of Yeshua. The Judeans were taunting him:

> "*Avraham avinu* died; you aren't greater than he, are you? Who do you think you are—someone greater than Avraham our father?"
> Yeshua answered, "Avraham, your father, was glad that he would see my day; then he saw it and was overjoyed."
> "Why, you're not yet fifty years old," the Judeans replied, "and you have seen Avraham?"
> Yeshua said to them, "Yes, indeed! Before Avraham came into being, I AM!" At this they picked up stones to throw at him" (John 8:56–59).

Why did these words of Yeshua evoke such a violent response? Surely it was because the hearers understood the sub-text.

In using the words "I AM," Yeshua was identifying himself with the God of Isra'el. He was claiming divinity. This was utterly unacceptable to Jewish people. It was then and, generally, it still is today. This is the issue that separates Messianic from non-Messianic Jews: who, and what, is Yeshua? Is he a prophet, even the greatest of the prophets? Or is he the divine Son of God?

> Can we join with Sha'ul in proclaiming:
>
> That in honor of the name given Yeshua,
> every knee will bow—
> in heaven, on earth and under the earth—
> and every tongue will acknowledge
> that Yeshua the Messiah is ADONAI
> to the glory of God the Father. (Phil.2:10–11)
>
> The question is still, "Who do you say that I am?"

For Thought

Believing that the holiness of God makes him altogether "other" can make him seem very distant, remote. At Sinai God commanded the people to erect the Tabernacle as a symbol of his presence among them. Everything about that tented structure seemed to cry out "Keep away; do not touch!" The gold, silver, and bronze furnishings and utensils spoke of God's glory; the fine white linen curtains embroidered in gold, purple, blue, and red spoke of God's holiness and beauty. Access, beyond the bronze altar of sacrifice, was limited to one tribe. Only the priestly family could enter the Holy Place. Only the High Priest might venture into the Most Holy Place, and that but once a year. How distant God's presence must have seemed to the ordinary Israelite.

The writer of the letter to early Messianic Jews must have had all this in mind, when he encouraged them with these words: "Let us confidently approach the throne from which God gives grace" (Heb. 4:16). He saw the Tabernacle and high priesthood as shadows of the reality to come that was Yeshua. Yeshua, he claimed, has gone right through into the presence of God, destroying the barriers through his death and resurrection. He has left the way open behind him, so to speak, and says to his followers, "Come on, follow me. It's all right. I've cleared it with my Father."

This means that we can now draw near into the very presence of *HaKadosh*, the holy God. That is a staggering thought, but the privilege is ours; it is real. We must, however, be mindful that the invitation comes to us from a holy God, whose name and character are utterly different from ours. It comes to us as an act of his grace, not of our deserving. We should never respond to the invitation carelessly or unworthily. We may approach confidently; we may never approach arrogantly, hypocritically, or lightly. Hear again the writer to the Hebrews:

> Therefore, let us approach the Holiest Place with a sincere heart, in the full assurance that comes from trusting—with our hearts sprinkled clean from a bad conscience and our bodies washed with pure water. (Heb. 10:22)

A Prayer

> Lord, I am amazed you are *El Shaddai*, the Almighty, yet you take note of me. You are ADONAI *Tzva'ot*, the Lord of hosts, yet you consent to use me in your service. You are *Av she baShamayim*, the heavenly Father, yet you tell me to call you my Father. You are *haKadosh*, the Holy One, yet you invite me to draw near to you. You are *Av haRakhamim*, the Father of mercies, and that is how you are able to accept me; for you have laid on your Son, my Savior Yeshua, the punishment for all the sin that separated me from you.
>
> Who is there who has ever been, or ever could be, remotely like you? You alone are my God, my Lord, my King, and my Deliverer.
>
> ADONAI! Our Lord! How glorious
> is your name throughout the earth! (Ps. 8:1)

I will praise you to the heights, my God, the king;
I will bless your name forever and ever.
Every day I will bless you;
I will praise your name forever and ever. . . .
ADONAI is close to all who call on him,
to all who sincerely call on him. . . .
My mouth will proclaim the praise of ADONAI;
all people will bless his holy name forever and ever.
(Ps. 145:1; 18; 21)

CHAPTER 6

Whose Kingdom Is Forever and Ever

מַלְכוּתוֹ לְעוֹלָם וָעֶד

Malkhuto L'Olam Va'ed

It is uncertain how early the custom began of inserting this sentence into the Sh'ma. Some have suggested that it was quite late. It may have been introduced into public worship during the last century or so before the Common Era as a protest against the political situation. The Hasmoneans had usurped the kingship that rightly belonged to the house of David, and the religious situation was in turmoil. The Sadducees, who were influential in the religious establishment, were denying the future life. These words may have been inserted as a tacit declaration affirming the Kingship of God and the reality of eternity.

Malkhuto l'olam va'ed (Whose kingdom is forever and ever) proclaims the eternity of God the King. The words echo the call of the Levites in the days of Nechemyah (Nehemiah): "Stand up, and bless ADONAI your God from everlasting to everlasting." They went on to link God's eternity with the praise of his name: "Let them say: 'Blessed be your glorious name, exalted above all blessing and praise!'" (Neh. 9:5).

Alternative Translations

As we have seen, there are several ways of translating these words. Some versions attach the word "glorious" to the name. Others attach it to the royalty and majesty of God, like this:

> Blessed be the name of his glorious kingdom forever and ever (Lamm, 69).
> Blessed is the name of his glorious majesty forever and ever (Donin, 146).

Kingship

An important feature of this sentence, whatever the translation, is the kingship—the eternal kingship—of God. Isra'el recognizes that kingship now. The day will surely come, wrote the prophet Z'kharyah (Zechariah), when "everyone remaining from all the nations that came to attack Yerushalayim [Jerusalem] will go up every year to worship the king, ADONAI-*Tzva'ot* [the LORD of Hosts]" (Zech. 14:16).

Towards the end of most synagogue services a well-known hymn is sung, which concludes with these two verses, declaring the eternal sovereignty of God:

> Lord of the world, King supreme
> Before anything was formed, He alone reigned.
> When by his will all things were created,
> His sovereign name was made known.

> And at the end, when all things cease to be
> The exalted God alone will still be King.
> He was, and He is,
> and He will be forever glorious. (*Adon Olam.* Budoff, 94)

Hertz wrote that the idea of the sovereignty of God was linked to the Sh'ma as early as the period of the second Temple, after the return from exile under Ezra. That, he said, is why the rabbis ordained that we should follow the first verse of the Sh'ma with the "*Barukh Shem.*" We are saying that there is only one God, and he is the supreme force for good in all the affairs of history. That good will ultimately triumph, because he is the reigning supreme King of kings (Hertz, *Authorised Daily Prayer Book with Commentary* 266).

This interpretation is in accord with the widely held Jewish belief that God's ultimate reign is to be in this world, not the next. It will happen when Messiah comes. Yes, God reigns eternally in the heavens; one day, however, he will reign right *here on earth*, through the Messiah, who will be recognized as king, *here on earth*, because he is of the royal house of David. So strong is this belief that Jewish people frequently cite it to combat the possibility of the Messiahship of Yeshua. How can Messiah/King have already come, when there is manifestly no reign of righteousness in the world? Klausner expresses the problem. Judaism, he says, is unequivocally concerned with this world. "It seeks...to amend this *world* by the kingdom of God" (Klausner, 405–06). He cited the *Alenu* Prayer:

> May we soon behold the glory of your might; when you remove the abominations from the earth and all idolatry is banished; when all the world will be made perfect under the reign of the Almighty.... May all the inhabitants of the world realize, and know, that every knee must bend and every tongue must swear allegiance to you. Lord our God, may they bend the knee and worship before you and give honor to the glory of your name. May they accept the yoke of your kingdom, and may you establish your reign over them quickly, forever and to eternity.... And it is said, "And the Lord shall be King over all the earth; on that day the Lord will be one and his name One."

The Talmud speaks of God as King—*our* King, our *only* King: "Beside thee we have no king, who redeems and saves...yea, we have no king but thee" (*Pes.* 18a). These words appear in the prayer called "The Blessing of Song," which we sing mainly at festivals, most notably towards the end of the Passover *seder*.

The prayers of penitence on *Yom Kippur* include multiple repetitions of the words, "*Avinu Malkheynu*" (Our Father, Our King). We stand before God the King. It is to him that we answer. We may owe allegiance and obedience to earthly governments, but the words, "We have no king but Caesar," declared by the chief priests at the trial of Yeshua before Pontius Pilate (John 19:15. NIV), were the ultimate blasphemy.

The *Kaddish*

There is a prayer that is particularly associated with times of mourning, though it is used at other times as well. The *Kaddish* (Sanctification) brings together the two ideas of God's name and God's Kingdom. It begins:

> Magnified and sanctified be his great name in the world which he created according to his will. And may he establish his kingdom during your life and during your days, and during the life

of all the house of Isra'el, speedily and in the near future, and
say Amen.
May his great name be blessed forever and ever.
Blessed, praised and glorified, exalted, extolled and honored,
adored and lauded be the name of the Holy One, blessed be
He, beyond all blessings and hymns, praises and songs that are
uttered in the world, and say, Amen. (Donin 219)

Yeshua

Yeshua, in what we know as "the Lord's Prayer," coupled the sanctification of God's name with the coming of his kingdom on earth.
He seems to be saying that our minds should dwell on God the
King and his concerns before we mention our own needs. Matthew
also records the prayer as concluding with the words: "For kingship, power and glory are yours forever" (Matt. 6:9–11). This is
very close to "Blessed be his name whose glorious kingdom is forever and ever."

Klausner was right to point out that Yeshua differed from the traditional view when he spoke of a kingdom not of this world, a
kingdom among and within God's people. Such an unearthly concept is extremely difficult for Jewish people to accept. This did not,
however, mean that Yeshua had lost sight of Yesha'yahu's vision of a
transformed world, with transformed relationships. Surely he saw
that the only way to a transformed world is through transformed
people. That is why no political system can ever deliver the perfect
society. The prophet expressed it in these words: "All of us are like
someone unclean, all our righteous deeds like menstrual rags" (Isa.
64:5(6)). Unredeemed human nature cannot change itself.

Yeshua offers this transformation. The sinner can be forgiven;
the alcoholic can be dry; the addict can be free. Your life and mine
can be places where the King-Messiah reigns. Yeshua taught that the
kingdom is here and now. This was his first message (Matt. 4:17).
Where Yeshua reigns, there is the kingdom. This is the good news
in the here and now, for individuals and for communities.

One day Yeshua will come again as the angel promised (Acts
1:11). His first coming was as a lowly king, in fulfillment of
Z'kharyah's words, "Your king is coming to you...humble—he's

riding on a donkey, yes, on a lowly donkey's colt" (Zech. 9:9). When he returns, it will be different. Then he will establish his kingdom of righteousness in all the earth as the Jewish prophets foretold. This is what believers in Yeshua anticipate. This is the good news for tomorrow. Death is not the end; evil will not triumph. One day it will be true to say:

> The kingdom of the world
> has become the Kingdom
> of our Lord and his Messiah,
> and he will rule forever and ever. (Rev. 11:15)

Sha'ul was a man with a passion. He lived only for the spreading of the kingdom as widely as possible among the generation of his time. However, he fixed his sights firmly on the kingdom to come. "If it is only for this life that we have put our hope in Messiah," he told the Corinthian believers, "we are more pitiable than anyone" (1 Cor. 15:19). We find his personal doxology in the letter to the believers in Rome:

> For from him and through him
> and to him are all things.
> To him be the glory forever! (Rom. 11:36)

This is what Yeshua the Messiah offers: Kingdom-transformation today; kingdom-perfection tomorrow.

For Thought

None of this is of any value as an abstract idea. It is as the rabbis saw concerning the declaration of the Sh'ma: a response is required. Yeshua had little time for theological arguments. He would challenge, "What about *you*?" "*You* need to do something about your life." "*You* need to be born again." "*You* need to take up your cross and follow me." The saying of the words, the intellectual acceptance of the dogma, are not enough. I have to immerse myself in the reality of kingdom living, and I need to be in a worshipping community that will help me to do that.

What is "kingdom living"? Quite simply, it is an attitude. A kingdom is the place where the king reigns. Who, or what, reigns in my life? Answer—the King. Who is the arbiter in my decision-making? Answer—the King. What is my reference-point? Answer—the King. What is my reason for being here? Answer—to serve and please the King. Whose smile do I want to see at the end of the day? Answer—the King's. That is kingdom living:

Yehudah HaLevy, twelfth century poet, expressed it like this: "To look at the face of my King—that is my only wish."

A key word for kingdom living is obedience. Again and again Moshe told the people to listen to God's words and obey them. The Lord would bless them "if you will listen to, observe and obey the mitzvot of ADONAI your God and not turn away from any of the words I am ordering you today" (Deut. 28:14).

Another key word is respect. A good monarch is loved—yes; obeyed—yes; but also held in honor. One is not "buddy-buddy" with the monarch. Any relationship is on his/her terms, and we are privileged to be allowed to approach royalty. God is incredibly gracious in allowing—even desiring—us to draw near to him and to enjoy a close relationship. We must never allow ourselves to lose sight of this truth. ADONAI Elohim is not my buddy. He is my King. I am his subject. As such, I love him; I obey him; I honor and respect him.

Does Yeshua say to you and me today: "What about *you*? Stop arguing about theological niceties among yourselves. Enough of this niggling criticism of one another. It is time to do something about allowing me to reign in your lives and in your communities."

How much can I honestly claim that Yeshua is the King in my life?

A Prayer

> I raise my eyes to you,
> whose throne is in heaven. (Ps. 123:1)

My Father, my King, I know that your rightful place is on the throne of my life, and that is where I want you to be. That is what is right for you, and best for me. I know this, but so many times I undermine your position. I compromise on priorities, and my allegiance falters. Others may not see this, but you know. O my Father, my King, always ready to forgive, I say again: "I have no King but you" (*Avinu Malkheynu*).

Sometimes, Lord, I become disheartened as I look at the state of the world. Injustice triumphs in the legal system; the profit motive holds sway; your beautiful planet is abused not stewarded; virtue and goodness are despised; evil is seen as good and good as evil. Only as I lift my eyes to you can I escape this downward pull on my spirit. Only as I walk in the light of your words can I experience the freedom and joy of kingdom life. Only as I look to the promises of your Word can I retain faith. Lord, I want to say to you now:

To the One sitting on the throne
and to the Lamb
belong praise, honor, glory and power
forever and ever. (Rev. 5:13)

Blessed be his glorious name forever,
and may the whole earth be filled with his glory. *Amen. Amen.*
(Ps. 72:19)

A Call
To Love

CHAPTER 7

And You Shall Love The Lord Your God

וְאָהַבְתָּ אֵת יהוה אֱלֹהֶיךָ

V'ahavta et ADONAI *Eloheycha*

"Choose life, so that you will live, you and your descendants, loving ADONAI your God, paying attention to what he says and clinging to him—for that is the purpose of your life!" (Deut. 30:19–20).

Ahavat HaShem (the love for God) is a fundamental concept in Judaism. That is why the rabbis have considered these words to be among the most significant in the whole *Tanakh* (Old Testament). Love, after all, is the highest level of relationship, and it is relationship that God wants with his people. He has forged a covenant with Isra'el from the days of Avraham—before Isra'el even existed—and covenant means relationship. God relates to his people in love, and love is the response for which he looks. Fear of punishment, hope for reward—these are present in our attitude to Almighty God, but at a lower level. Pure love is what God seeks from us. We do indeed fear him, and that fear may make us shrink from evil doing; but our response to his care and his goodness to us is love.

God has told us, in lofty terms, who he is in himself, and who he is in relation to Isra'el. The context of the Sh'ma is the closing days of the desert wanderings. God has revealed himself as the One who saw our pain, heard our cry, cared about us, and came down to deliver us (Exod. 3:7–9). That is love. Isra'el's love is the natural response to who God is and what he has done for us.

One might wonder that God is at all concerned that we should love him. Is he, then, so vulnerable that he needs our love? Lamm suggests that God is actually lonely, that his oneness implies solitude. Our hearts reach out to him in that loneliness, and that reaching out is our response of love (Lamm, 122).

God is to Be Loved Through Us

The rabbis have always taught that pure love is more than emotional feeling. The Talmud tells us that this command means we are to conduct ourselves in such a way as to cause other people to love God. The purpose is that because of us, the name of heaven will become beloved (*Yoma* 86a). The love for God, therefore, embraces others. We cannot say we love him and yet not impact the lives of our fellow men for good. Such love is not an affair of the emotions; it is a matter of practical living and social relationships. We need to be in good standing among our fellows—even be loved by them—so that love will be reflected onto God (Montefiore and Loewe, 558). This is part of God's strategy to use his people as a mirror image of himself. For instance, he speaks to the prophet Yechezk'el (Ezekiel) of the day when "before their [the nations'] eyes, I am set apart through you to be regarded as holy" (Ezek. 36:23). God's intention is that the nations will look at Isra'el, and what they see will arouse in them a desire for him.

Love and Fear

Jewish thought sees a connection between love of God and fear of God. True love will embrace true fear. The interpretation of this teaching, however, varies. Orthodox teaching has been that love and fear of God cannot be separated. To be a good Jew is to love and fear him in equal measure, and to do so wholeheartedly. This love and this fear, for the Orthodox Jew, are identified with the study of Torah and the performance of the mitzvot.

The philosopher Maimonides thought differently. He rated love above fear. Love, he said, is stronger because it is positive; it causes us to reach out to the Creator. Fear works negatively; it causes us to shrink away.

Mystical thought is different again. The Hasidim sought to cultivate love and fear as separate aims. They are the two wings of religious experience. Hasidism even developed a whole system of prayer techniques in order to induce love and fear of God. Hasidism was about the search for piety, and the road to piety is through a life that is transparently filled with both love and fear of God.

The Study of Creation

Maimonides had a rationalistic approach to religion. He believed that love and fear of God are to be attained through the study of Creation: "When a man contemplates his great and wondrous deeds and creations, and sees in them his unequaled and infinite wisdom, he immediately loves and praises and exalts Him" (*Mishneh* Torah: *Hilhkot Yesodei ha* Torah 2:2). For Maimonides, education meant more than Torah and Talmud study. His "contemplation" of Creation meant a proper study of what we would now call the natural sciences. He was a far more broadly educated man than was usual in contemporary Jewish society, firmly maintaining that increase in knowledge of God through his works would lead to increase in love for him.

The Study of Torah

Donin is wary of Maimonides' teaching here. In the light of today's prevailing current of skepticism he prefers the safety of Torah. For him the direct route to God is through the intensive study of Torah. Only Torah, he asserts, can lead us into awe and love for God (Donin, 150).

Prayer

> Love for God is one of the main themes of the *Hasidim*. A *Hasid*, indeed, is one who is filled with love for God. That is true piety. He aims to achieve this love through prayer as well as through Torah study. Jacobs quotes Rabbi Shneor Zalman of Liady: "A man must reflect on this theme [God's greatness and glory] until the contemplative soul is awakened to love the Lord's name, to cleave to Him and to his Torah and greatly to desire his commandments" (Jacobs, *Hasidic Prayer* 18). One can see here contemplative prayer as the starting point, leading to Torah study, and so on to love and obedience. Traditional thought has been wary of this somewhat introspective approach. It makes Torah

study the starting point, obedience to Torah the goal. That is, itself, our way of showing love to God. Eliezer Azikri, the 16th century mystic, expressed it like this:

> Beloved of my soul, merciful Father, draw Your servant after You to do Your will. (Eliezer Azriki. Carmi, 471)

Evidences of Love

Traditional Judaism teaches that one shows love for God by meticulous obedience to the commandments of Torah. This is a matter of self-discipline—of the will. Plaut sees such obedience as a matter of loyalty, without which love will wither (Plaut, 1370). There is also, however, space for *devekut* (devotion). Friedlander put it like this: "Love of God...means the constant longing for communion with Him, feeling happy and joyful when with Him, but unhappy and miserable when without Him" (Friedlander, 274). Such yearning for fellowship with God is expressed in Psalm 42: "Just as a deer longs for running streams, God, I long for you." Moses Hayim Luzzatto, in the 18th century, put it like this:

> To love God is to be so imbued with the love of God that we are impelled, of our own accord, to give Him pleasure, so to speak, in the same way as a child sometimes feels moved to give pleasure to his father and mother. (Leviant, 555)

> The prime evidence of love is obedience, a striving to please the beloved.

The ultimate in love-relationships—marriage—is an illustration of the relationship between God and Isra'el. Such love has to be mutual (Lamm, 122–23). Love demands and begets the response of love. We, as the people of Isra'el, must love him because we are in covenant relationship to him; he *our* God, we *his* people (ADONAI *Eloheynu*—the LORD *our* God). I, as an individual Jew, must love him, because he is the Lord *my* God (ADONAI *Eloheycha*—the Lord *thy* God). We are bound together in a relationship whose bonding power is love.

Yeshua

Yeshua, when asked which was the most important of the mitzvot, had no hesitation in replying. "You are to love ADONAI your God with all your heart and with all your soul and with all your strength" (Matt. 22:35–37). Those who were trying to trap him could hardly find fault with that!

He also accorded with traditional thinking in teaching that love is demonstrated by deeds. "If you love me, you will keep my commands," he taught his disciples (John 14:15). "Whoever has my commands and keeps them is the one who loves me" (John 14:21).

Yeshua made a connection between love and forgiveness, using the actions of a woman of poor reputation to illustrate the point (Luke 7:36–50). Her extravagant generosity proved the depth and boundless extent of her love. It also, however, demonstrated the comprehensiveness of the forgiveness she had received and the gratitude she longed to express. Love is a reflection of relationship, and in the matter of my relationship with God it is sin that stands in the way. When I am forgiven, that sin removed, I am free to feel, express, and receive love.

Love, the Response to Love

For disciples of Yeshua, love for God is a response to Yeshua's dying for us. It is the only acceptable response. "We ourselves love now because he loved us first," wrote Yochanan (1 John 4:19). Love, for us, is not only the response to our national deliverance three and a half millennia ago—though that is an important factor. It does not spring only out of the study of the Scriptures—though that may be a contributing factor. It does not find its source in contemplative prayer—though that may help its development. Love is the spontaneous response of a person who has received unmerited forgiveness, at enormous cost, and who knows himself—herself—to be transformed by the life that Yeshua died to purchase.

The heart of the Good News of Yeshua is, "God so loved the world that he gave his only and unique Son, so that everyone who trusts in him may have eternal life" (John 3:16). How can we not love him?

For Thought

Love is a very personal thing. The people of *Isra'el* express that love together when, in synagogue and home, they remember God's actions on their behalf in times past. This is particularly so at the festival times. At *Pesach* (Passover) we give thanks for the deliverance from Egypt; at *Shavuot* (Pentecost) we remember the giving of Torah; at *Sukkot* (Tabernacles) we remember the years spent in the desert; at *Hanukkah* we rejoice in the miracle of the oil and the cleansing of the Temple. This expression of community love, however, is the sum of the love of each individual in the group. He is *our* God, but he is also *my* God.

In all congregations, both Jewish and gentile, is it possible that the worship may feel good, but perhaps some people there are merely passengers? The object of public worship is not to work up emotional feeling, but to please God. He will be pleased if such worship builds up each person's love for him, stimulates each person to go out and live the way he wants them to live. The command is still "to love ADONAI your God, to follow all his ways and to cling to him" (Deut. 11:22).

The crunch comes when I am alone, in privacy. I am a forgiven sinner; God's love has touched and changed my heart. How much, though, do I cultivate that love, give it space to grow? How high on my list of priorities is the development of that relationship with him, which finds expression in the words "*My* Lord and *my* God"? What price am I prepared to pay in response to him who first loved me and gave himself for me?

During the Great Plague in England (1665–66), there was a village called Eyam that, when the disease came among them, decided to cut itself off totally in order to contain the deadly infection. This meant certain death for many who might otherwise have escaped by running away. They took an oath together that they would do this, for the sake of others in surrounding communities. They saw this as following in the footsteps of Yeshua, who died on the Cross for them.

In the formal taking of that oath they were responding to God's love in a way that made sense to them, and they were able to encourage one another by a knowledge that this was something they were all in together. That, however hard and soul-searching it was,

was only the beginning—the easy part. Afterwards came the long months of living out the vow. They watched and waited, not knowing who would live and who would die. In some families there was only one survivor. Some families were wiped out altogether. In all, 260 people died in that small community. Those months were the hard part, yet they remained true to their vow. The sacrifice of the Eyam villagers has gone into English history.

How deeply has God's love touched my heart? How much hardship and pressure would my responding love survive? How long a time of darkness will it endure? How much pain will it overcome?

We need to nurture our love for the Lord today, to invest our resources in him while we can. Tomorrow the crash may come and the darkness be upon us. Then it will be too late. That will be the time for drawing upon our investment.

One last thought. Many people believe that love arises spontaneously. However, in the words of the Sh'ma, God *commands* us to love him. That means we are to love him as an act of obedience. This calls for an act of the will. Love, in the modern western world, has been cheapened. We give up if it gets hard. God knows that loving him will sometimes get hard. We shall not always feel like it. When that happens, we need to grit our teeth and keep on loving him by the way we live and by what we do. Loyalty and perseverance will rekindle love.

A Prayer

Lord, it is easy for me to say the words, "I love you." It is easier still to sing them. Forgive me the times I say and sing them from an empty heart just because everyone else is doing it. Forgive me the times I say and sing them when my life is not being lived in obedience to you. You have done so much for me and your forgiveness is beyond my understanding. Please grow your love in me; this is not something I can work at on my own. Blessed are you, O Lord my God, who has loved me with an everlasting love.

CHAPTER 8

With All Your Heart

בְּכָל לְבָבְךָ

B'kol l'vav'cha

We have already seen that God desires for us to love him. Now he tells us to love him with all our heart. What does this mean?

The Bible sees the heart as the essential center, the hub, and the core of our being. It is the seat of self-consciousness. The writer of Proverbs speaks of the heart knowing the pains and joys that cannot be fully shared with anyone else (Prov. 14:10).

The traditional authorities agree that the heart is a complex organ. It is the seat of intellect, emotion, and attitude, though it is not easy to differentiate between these three aspects. Jewish belief is that this is true of both biblical and talmudic teaching. It is with the heart that we think, feel, and make decisions.

The Intellect

Bahya (Ben Asher Ben Halawa) taught that "It is the intellect that draws the soul to God and evokes love" (Lamm, 108).

Maimonides went further, taking a rationalistic view of love. He saw it as an altogether mental response, linked to knowledge. According to this view, one can only obey the command to love God with the heart by immersing oneself in study. The way to achieve love of God, he felt, is to understand him, and such understanding comes through studying Torah. He felt it was impossible to love God without understanding, knowing, him. "One loves the Holy One only with the mind, thus knowing him; for love is in accordance with knowledge; if little then little, if much then much" (*Mishneh* Torah: *Hilkhot Teshuvah* 110:3).

The prophet Yesha'yahu (Isaiah) spoke of the heart as the seat, not just of knowledge, but of understanding (6:10). The Talmud likewise teaches that "The heart gives understanding" (*Shabb.* 33b). We should pray that our hearts will give us understanding as we meditate on God (*Ber.* 17a).

The thought-life stems from the heart. The heart discerns, perceives, and knows truth. It can learn and profit from experience. It remembers, forgets, and forms convictions (*Jewish Encyclopedia*, volume 6, 295, "Heart"). In spite of all God had done for the people, Moshe had to rebuke them, at the end of the day: "To this day ADONAI has not given you a heart to understand, eyes to see or ears to hear!" (Deut. 29: 3(4)) Sometimes the Bible uses the expression "He said in his heart." The clear meaning is "He thought." David prayed that the thoughts of his heart might be acceptable to God (Ps. 19:14–15).

We are, therefore, to love God with our intellect, understanding, and thinking. This means, taught Hirsch, that we strive to reach out to God, using all the mental capacities God has given us.

The Emotions

The heart is seen as the source of all layers of human feeling. It encompasses hunger and thirst, courage, hatred, pride, deceit, sorrow, joy, reverence, and remorse (*Jewish Encyclopedia,* vol. 6 195–96 "Heart"). The Talmud echoes the writer of Proverbs, telling us that it is the heart that knows bitterness (*Yoma* 83a).

Judaism recognizes love as a powerful emotion. It is, therefore, important that no other love should stand before our love of God. This is what it means to love God with *all* the heart. One must not ask him to share one's heart with anyone or anything else. Rashi tells the story of *Yosef* (Joseph) falling on his father's neck when they met in Egypt after so many years. Apparently Ya'akov did not return the embrace. Why not? Rashi explains that Ya'akov was reciting the Sh'ma at the time. He felt he should give this rising tide of love for his long-lost son to God, so that his love for a human being might not be greater than his love for God. The aim, the ideal, is that one's heart should feel only one overpowering attraction, and that is for the heavenly Father. This means a total absorption with the loved One—God. These lines express it most beautifully:

> Ever since you were the home of love for me
> my love has lived where you have lived. (Judah Halevy. *The Home of Love*. Carmi 333)

The Will

The heart is also seen as the "seat of volition" (*Jewish Encyclopedia*, volume 6, 295 "Heart"). We find authority for this view in Daniel 1:8. The literal Hebrew wording is "Dani'el purposed in his heart." The Talmud explains that Dani'el made a deliberate choice (*Avodah Zara* 36a). The CJB has "Dani'el resolved." When the people were setting about the building of the Tabernacle in the desert, they brought free-will offerings for its construction and beautification. We read that "every man and woman of the people of Isra'el whose heart impelled him to contribute to any of the work ADONAI had ordered through Moshe brought it to ADONAI as a voluntary offering" (Exod. 35:29). It was within their hearts that they made the decision to give.

This ought not to be a strange concept to us. We speak of "a change of heart," meaning a change of mind, a decision to alter direction. That is what *teshuvah* (repentance) is: a change of heart; a decision of the will to change direction.

What is it, then, to love God with all the will? It means making a conscious decision to love God with everything, holding nothing back. What one actually *feels* like has nothing to do with the matter. Donin explains why three words appear in the *Siddur* just before the Sh'ma. When praying alone one should say the words *El melech ne'eman* (God, faithful king) before reciting the Sh'ma. Why are these words there? They bring the total number of words in the Sh'ma to 248. That is proverbially the number of parts of the body. The worshipper is dedicating his entire body to God's service.

An understanding heart is a hearing heart. We make a decision to listen to God. *Shlomo* (Solomon) asked God for an understanding heart. Tradition interprets this as "a hearing heart" (*Jewish Encyclopedia*, volume 6, 296 "Heart"). Years after *Shlomo*, God made the point to Yesha'yahu that seeing with the eyes and hearing with the ears are sterile unless accompanied by understanding with the heart. They alone do not lead to fruit, to action (Isa. 6:10). God will not tolerate the "haughty of eye and proud of heart" (*Arachin* 15b). The Talmud describes a heart that listens and responds when God speaks as a "tender heart" (*Sukk.* 38b).

Sometimes we find the expression "circumcision of the heart." Those who are disobedient to Torah are "uncircumcised in heart" (*Yoma* 71b). There is a prayer in *B'rakhot*: "Circumcise our hearts to fear thee" (*Ber.* 29a).

Prayer is one way we demonstrate love of God. Prayer is difficult. There has to be an effort of the will. The Talmud states, "When a man prays he should direct his heart toward heaven" (*Ber.* 31a). Not everyone has the same capacity for understanding or for prayer and study. Here is a word of encouragement: "It is the same whether a man offers much or little, so long as he directs his heart to heaven" (*Men.* 110a).

Yetzer hatov and Yetzer harah

Jewish tradition holds that the human heart is the site of two conflicting tendencies: the *yetzer hatov* (the good urge) and the *yetzer harah* (the bad urge). The whole of life is a contest between these two urges. We are constantly torn between the good and the evil. Our higher desire is to be positive, constructive, but we find ourselves drawn into negative, destructive situations. We long to be noble, deserving of honor and respect, but find ourselves partaking in unwholesome activities.

This means that, although we are in a moral battle, there is no doctrine of original sin to make the outcome inevitable, Success and goodness are as possible as failure and sin. We simply have to do battle—constant battle— with the impulse that drags us down. There have been differing views about how this doctrine affects our ability to love God with all the heart. Some have taught that it is possible to love God with *both* these urges (*Ber.* 54a). The way to do this is by sublimation and redirection of the *yetzer harah*. Others have said that we must fight and overcome the *yetzer harah*, either converting it into a force for good or by simply suppressing it.

Others again believe that the *yetzer harah* is an intrinsically evil part of human nature. We must subdue and even destroy it. It is in that confrontation and destruction of the evil within that we can claim to be loving God with the whole heart. This view has seemed to some to be the only way to make sense of the evil that was the Holocaust.

Morals

The heart will direct our morals. The choice to follow the *yetzer harah* or the *yetzer hatov* will decide whether we lead moral or immoral lives. We have a choice. We make that choice by the exercise of the will. Solomon, the writer of Proverbs, in a passage about morals, directs us: "Above everything else, guard your heart; for it is the source of life's consequences" (Prov. 4:23).

We have a choice all the time. However, if we persist in following the direction of the *yetzer harah*, our conscience will become blunted. In the words of the Talmud: "Sin dulls the heart of man" (*Yoma* 39a). The Bible holds out the threat of an even worse consequence of hardening the heart against God. There came such a time for Pharaoh. He persisted in hardening his heart until there came a time when God hardened it for him.

The Scriptures seem to take a pessimistic view of men's hearts. Early in man's story, "ADONAI saw that the people on earth were very wicked, that all the imaginings of their hearts were always of evil only" (Gen. 6:5). Moshe saw the need for his people to circumcise their hearts (Deut. 10:16). David grieved that his heart was unclean (Ps. 51:10(12)). Yirmeyahu described the heart as "more deceitful than anything else and mortally sick" (Jer. 17:9). God showed *Yechezk'el* that the people's hearts were rock-hard (Ezek. 36:26).

When God looks down upon us, does he see anything but hardness of heart?

Yeshua

Intellect, emotions, will: of these three areas of personality it seems that Yeshua was most concerned with the third. To him, knowledge was the path to doing. Blessing is for those who obey his words rather than for those who simply hear them (Matt. 7:24–27). He never seemed to look for or welcome an emotional response. He knew men's hearts and saw right through the shallow attraction and instant response to the inner person, the motives, and the depth.

When it comes to the will, however, Yeshua has more to say. He called men and women to follow him and keep on following; to set their hands to the plough and not look back. He demanded discipline of the thought-life; what comes out of the mouth, issuing from the heart, is more important than what goes into it (Matt. 15:11). Sin originates in the recesses of the heart, where the intention forms, before any unclean action is taken (Matt. 5:28).

The New Covenant call to repentance was not emotional; it demanded a decision, an act of will. The call to follow was not emotional; it demanded a decision, a change of life's direction. Yeshua promised grace and power, but first the heart must respond.

Sha'ul

If we are looking for an intellectual approach, Sha'ul is our man. God may not have chosen a "Pharisee of the Pharisees" to bring salvation, but he certainly chose one to proclaim that salvation, and to explain it. I must confess that I find much of Sha'ul's writings mentally demanding—even exhausting. However, I never cease to marvel at his ability to tailor his teaching to the needs and background of each different community. He laid his considerable intellectual ability and rabbinical expertise at the feet of the Messiah, for the benefit of his people. To the Greeks he was able to be a cultured classicist. To Jewish people he was a learned Pharisee. Not everyone has those kinds of abilities. Sha'ul had them, and he used them to the utmost. That was his way of loving.

Yochanan (John)

We have to turn to Yochanan for the emotional dimension. Sha'ul's words may come to us like a lecture; Yochanan's come as a song. To use an English expression, they "touch the heart," even bringing tears to the eyes. This man, you think, *feels* love; he evokes the *feeling* of love in me. The teaching is there; the demands of love are there; but something intangible melts my heart and draws me to Yeshua the Messiah.

How gracious of God to use every conceivable means to draw us to him!

For Thought

Yeshua impacts our hearts in more than one way. We need to satisfy ourselves intellectually that he is "the Way, the Truth and the Life," as he claimed to be (John 14:6). He too has expectations: he requires of us a surrender of the will—he must be Lord. Then, at some stage, we should expect to *feel* something. For most people that feeling begins with a sense of peace and joy. These three elements—understanding, feeling, and willing—do not happen in the same order for everyone. For me, surrender came first, followed very quickly by feeling. After that, intellectual satisfaction was a long, hard graft. For many of you, intellectual conviction had to come first. For some it was the experience, perhaps totally unexpected, of being touched by, hearing, or even seeing, a vision of Yeshua. Others will have been challenged by the call to repentance, perhaps by a crisis, even a broken life.

For all of us, however, our love of God must include the will and the mind as well as the emotions. Otherwise our love will be like human love: fickle, changeable, unpredictable, "like a morning cloud, like dew that disappears quickly" (Hos. 6:4). When we feel cold and dry—and we shall feel cold and dry at times—we need our knowledge of him, the memories of what he has done for us in the past. We need a storehouse of his teaching to keep us firm and true. We need the grit and determination to carry on, to stick with him though he feels distant. How we do that is the true measure of our love.

Some of us are naturally emotional and demonstrative. We should guard against intellectual laziness. The Holy Spirit is no substitute for the Bible. He recalls the Bible to our mind according to our need, but will he recall passages we have never read?

Some of us, on the other hand, are more cerebral. We need to feel in control of ourselves, to understand before we commit ourselves. We should guard against arrogance and coldness, and a critical spirit. Others may not have our intellectual ability, but they perhaps have a warmth of personality, an ability to empathize with others, that we lack.

God in his wisdom and grace gave us different personalities. He does not ask us to be people we are not. He asks us to love him with what we are.

A Prayer

Lord God, my Creator, you gave me a mind and a will so that I am not an automaton. You gave me the power to choose whether to love you or not. Keep me firm in my love when I feel nothing. Keep me true to you when it would be easier to slide back. Without you I would be at the mercy of my emotions within and the winds of change in the world around. It is good, therefore, for me to declare with Sha'ul: "I am sure of this: that the One who began a good work among you will keep it growing until it is completed on the Day of the Messiah Yeshua" (Phil. 1:6).

> My God, when I feel so downcast,
> I remind myself of you ...
> My soul, why are you so downcast?
> Why are you groaning inside me?
> Hope in God, since I will praise him again
> for being my Savior and God. (Ps. 42:6(7); 11(12))

Blessed are you, O Lord our God, who made us all different, yet all with the capacity to love you.

CHAPTER 9

With All Your Being

בְּכָל נַפְשְׁךָ

B'kol nafsh'cha

"The blood is the life [*nefesh*]" (Deut. 12:23).

Five different Hebrew words are commonly translated into English as 'soul': *ruach, nefesh, neshamah, chayyah, yechidah*. In the Sh'ma we find *nefesh*. It is not always easy to define the difference between these terms, because Hebrew thought does not deal with clear-cut categories. The Western world, heavily influenced by Greek philosophy, has been accustomed to dividing the human personality into body, mind, and spirit. Such categories are foreign to the Hebrew mind.

Not surprisingly, therefore, it is difficult to define the word *nefesh* with any precision. In its verbal form it can mean "to take breath, to be refreshed." The Creation story tells us that man "became a living being [*nefesh*]" when God "breathed into his nostrils the breath of life" (Gen. 2:7). With God's breath in him he became a living, breathing person. In Leviticus 2:1 we find *nefesh* translated as "anyone"; that is to say, a person, a human being. Cohen turns to the words of Deuteronomy chapter 12, quoted above; *nefesh*, he says, equals blood, equals life. The Rabbinic Anthology broadens the definition: *nefesh* is the seat of passions, appetites, and personality. It is the soul, the life; it is the person himself (Montefiore, 272).

Life

Put simply, the presence of *nefesh* gives life; its absence indicates lack of life. Some have said that all animal life has *nefesh*, because there is no life without it, but usually it signifies human life. It is the *nefesh* that casts us in the image of God, and separates us from all other animal life. Human beings have an affinity with their Maker, and that sets us above all other creatures. This difference carries with it certain challenges and responsibilities. There are implications of conscience. "The soul is the spiritual force within man which raises him above an animal existence, inspires him with ideals, and prompts him to choose the good and reject the evil" (Cohen 83).

The Talmud teaches that the soul exists before it inhabits a body; it waits in a place called the *Guph*. Likewise it continues after leaving the body at death. Abigail came to David, seeking mercy and conciliation, with these words: "Even if someone comes along searching for you and seeking your life [*nefesh*], your life [*nefesh*] will be bound in the bundle of life with ADONAI your God" (1 Sam. 25:29). There is always the hope that the *nefesh* of the godly will be "bound in the bundle of life" after death.

Body and Soul

The rabbis have given some thought to the relationship between the body and the soul. The Talmud teaches that the soul bears the same relationship to the body that God bears toward the created universe. The soul fills the whole body as God fills the whole universe. The soul nourishes the whole body as God nourishes the whole universe. The soul dwells in the inmost part of the body as God dwells in the inmost part of the universe (*Ber.* 10a):

> As long as you live, you are akin to the living God: just as He is invisible, so are you. Since your Creator is pure and flawless, know that you too are pure and perfect. The Mighty One upholds the heavens on his arm, as you uphold the mute body. (*The Soul and its Maker.* Solomon Ibn Gabirol. Carmi 315)

One cannot, therefore, separate body and soul; neither are they hostile to one another. They fit so well together that Talmud describes the body as "the scabbard of the soul" (*San.* 108a). "The body is not the prison of the soul, but its medium for development and improvement" (*Jewish Encyclopedia* Volume 11, 473, "Soul").

Many Christians experience what they see as conflict between the soul and the body. They feel that "the flesh" wars against "the spirit," asserting a constant downward pull. Historically this has led some to believe it right to punish and subjugate the flesh, to deny its natural appetites. Jewish people are ever optimistic. They recognize the conflict, but see it as an opportunity for growth. The "flesh" and its appetites are God-given. They are not to run out of control, but they are for our use and enjoyment.

The Soul is Pure

Traditional Judaism does not recognize the doctrine of original sin. The Talmud directs us to pray, on awakening, these words:

> My God, the soul which Thou hast placed in me is pure. Thou hast fashioned it in me, Thou didst breathe it into me, and Thou preservest it within me and Thou wilt one day take it from me and restore it to me in the time to come. So long as the soul is within me I give thanks unto Thee, O Lord, my God, and the God of my fathers, Sovereign of all worlds, Lord of all souls. Blessed art Thou, O Lord, who restorest souls to dead corpses. (*Ber.* 60b)

The belief is that the Holy One, blessed be he, is pure. Being pure, he would of course only bestow on his creatures a pure soul. Each individual, therefore, starts with a clean slate, so to speak. Each day offers a new, fresh, unsullied beginning. It is our responsibility to keep that soul pure, to "preserve it in purity," throughout the day (*Nid.* 30b).

This means that Jewish holy men and women do not start "in the red," having to battle their way out of sin and debt. They start "in the black," and devote their efforts to remaining so. "The character of a life depends upon the care which the individual devotes to keeping his soul pure and unstained" (Cohen, 81).

A person's soul is a most precious commodity. There is a delightful tradition concerning the soul and *Shabbat*. It says that on the eve of every *Shabbat* God gives one an extra soul, just for the duration of *Shabbat*. This means that the soul will have heightened powers, and *Shabbat* will be properly observed and enjoyed.

Blood

Two doctrines result from the connection between *nefesh* and blood. One comes from Deuteronomy 12: 23 and forbids the eating of blood. "Take care not to eat the blood, for the blood is the life [*nefesh*], and you are not to eat the life [*nefesh*] with the meat." Jewish law totally forbids the consuming of any blood.

The other doctrine concerns our attitude to human life. The shedding of blood, that is the taking of a life, is forbidden. God has planted the soul within each person, and it is not for us to separate that soul from its body, "to deprive this Divine spirit in man of its bodily frame" (Hirsch, 223).

Martyrdom

What does it mean to love the Lord with all my *nefesh*? Rabbi Akiba was in no doubt about this, as he recited the Sh'ma while suffering a horrendous death under torture:

> All my days I have been troubled by this verse, 'with all thy soul', [which I interpret] 'even if He takes thy soul'. I said: When shall I have the opportunity of fulfilling this? Now that I have the opportunity shall I not fulfill it? (*Ber.* 61b)

The Jerusalem Talmud adds these words:

> I have loved him with all my heart and I have loved him with all my possessions, but I was not tested as to my soul. Now that I have reached "all your soul," and the time for the reading of the Sh'ma has arrived, I shall not be distracted from loving him! That is why I recite—and smile.

According to Akiba, then, loving God with all the soul means suffering, and remaining true under, martyrdom.

Akiba's story has, of course, influenced the tradition. The rabbis have accepted his interpretation as being the plain meaning of the words. It is not clear, however, whether one actually has to endure martyrdom, or just be prepared to do so. Some would say that the intention is sufficient. As we recite the words, we are proclaiming our readiness to endure martyrdom. The *Hasidim* went further. The true *tzaddik*, they taught, will serve the Lord in every way possible, even if it should mean giving up his own life—or even the lives of his nearest and dearest!

The question is not theoretical. Martyrdom has, indeed, been a common experience in Jewry. The rabbis in Germany even felt it necessary to formulate a special *b'rakhah* (blessing) to be made by those facing it:

> Blessed art Thou, O Lord our God, King of the Universe, who hast sanctified us by Thy commandments and bade us love Thee with all our heart and with all our soul, and to sanctify Thy glorious and awful name in public. Blessed art Thou, O Lord, Who sanctifiest Thy name amongst the many. (Hertz, *Deuteronomy* 106–107)

All of Me

What does it mean to love God with all the soul? The *Hasidim* wanted to give this command a broader meaning than simply martyrdom. Martyrdom, after all, is not for everyone; and who can know how prepared they are until the eventuality happens? The Maharal, Rabbi Judah Loew of Prague, who influenced the early Hasidic movement, taught on this subject. He pointed out that the command to love God comes immediately after the declaration of who God is. That means we have a *reason* to love him, and it indicates the nature of the love required. It has to be more than emotional. We have stated that God is altogether other—unique. Our love for him, therefore, is to be altogether other—different—from our love for one another. It is a love that acknowledges him as the core of our life, and must be a love that offers itself in totality. When we say these words we put ourselves under an obligation to be more than superficial in our religious practice. We are undertaking to offer ourselves in totality to the Creator who is the only God.

This means that loving God with the whole *nefesh* is going to involve the whole being. Nothing can be withheld; nothing can be shared with any other god. God is alone. There can be no competition.

More modern, less traditional teachers have also given this matter some thought. The *Siddur Lev Chadash* tells us that "Religion should not merely give us hours of devotion; our whole life should be filled with devotion, for God looks down upon us always. And religion does not set before us isolated tasks; our whole life should be our task, for God speaks to us every day" (*Siddur Lev Chadash* 1).

Such a demand is based on reason. That reason is, as the *Hasidim* taught, the otherness, the awesomeness, of God. To love him with all the *nefesh* is to acknowledge the reality of the situation. It springs from a sense of awe, of wonder, a realization that we are part of a cosmic mystery.

To love God with all the *nefesh* is to offer up to him the whole of our being, our personality, and our life.

Yeshua

Yeshua not only taught the steadfast persistence of real love. He lived it. Love of his Father motivated him to submit to the human condition, the Jerusalem road, and the Gethsemane agony. Love of mankind led him to give himself to the uttermost, knowing at every stage what was going to come next. The words, "Not what I want, but what you want" (Matt. 26:39) are surely the ultimate example of what real love is. This love had no limits, no qualifications. It was totally self-giving. Yeshua demanded that his followers leave everything and everyone to be his *talmidim*, and he had the right to make that demand. He had said that the measure of love is in being prepared to lay down one's life for the beloved, and he himself did just that. Many of those followers, too, would love him with all their soul, even unto martyrdom.

For Thought

God made clear, through the teachings of the prophet Hosea, the ends to which his love would drive him in terms of forgiveness, acceptance, and a setting aside of the past. What man, in that society, would take back a wife who had been persistently and publicly unfaithful? God, however, does just that for Isra'el. His motive force is love.

It is in the life—and, crucially, the death—of Yeshua, however, that we see his full love demonstrated. It is a demonstration that is clearly foreshadowed in the *Tanakh*. The words of the gospel are explicit: "God so loved the world that he gave his only and unique Son, so that everyone who trusts in him may have eternal life" (John 3:16). That giving of God's Son meant death: "No one has greater love than a person who lays down his life for his friends" (John 15:13). The Son of Man came "to give his life as a ransom for many" (Matt. 20:28).

Why should we love Messiah Yeshua? Because he is who he is: God's Son, "the very expression of God's essence" (Heb. 1:3). Why should we love him? Because he has done what he has done, in order that we might know forgiveness and have life:

> And when he appeared as a human being,
> he humbled himself still more
> by becoming obedient even to death—
> death on a stake as a criminal! (Phil. 2: 7–8)

Dying was not just a result of Yeshua's life and ministry. It *was* that life and ministry. He stepped into the human condition for that express purpose. The whole exercise was love with all his *nefesh*; all his life, his humanity. In his incarnation he gave up everything that was his by right as being divine. In the shedding of his blood he gave everything that was his by right as being human. He has, therefore, the right to demand everything in return. What price, set beside the price he paid, can be too high for us to pay? How can we hesitate when he seems to ask so much? Many of us have known hostility from family when we committed our loves to Messiah. It has been hard. It still is hard. He knows. He has been there, and much further.

A Prayer

What can it mean for me, my Lord and my God, to love you with all my being? Sometimes I think I do not know the first thing about love. I am driven by my feelings, by my appetites, by my need to understand. Take me deeper, O my Lord, into the world of this kind of love. May the same mind be in me that was in Yeshua, who loved to the uttermost.

Blessed are you, O Lord my God, King of the universe, who commands me to have the same attitude as Messiah Yeshua, and to love you with all my being.

CHAPTER 10

With All Your Resources

בְּכָל מְאֹדֶךָ

B'kol m'odecha

We have seen that loving the Lord our God with all the heart (*l'vav'cha*) means loving him with the will as well as with the emotions. This is a love to which we must bring all our mental capacities. Loving the Lord our God with all the being (*nafsh'cha*) means loving him even to the place of the ultimate sacrifice—martyrdom. We have to love him with all our whole personality—with all that we are. What is there, then, to add to these high expectations? What can it mean, to love the Lord our God with all our strength, our resources (*m'odecha*)?

M'od

The word *m'od* is often translated in the Bible as "very," or "ever." When God looked at his Creation, at every stage he saw it to be "*tov*" (good). However, we read in Genesis 1:31 that at the end of the sixth day he looked at the complete picture and proclaimed it to be "*tov m'od*" (very good). The same word describes the anger of Kayin (Cain) when he saw that God had rejected him and his offering (Gen. 4:5). He was *very* angry. We see the same word again in Psalm 46:1(2), where the Psalmist praises God for being not just a help in trouble, but also "an ever-present help in trouble."

Genesis 7:19 conveys the same sense of "very-ness": "The water overpowered the earth mightily [*m'od*]." God used the same word to enlarge Avraham's vision concerning the extent of the blessing he had in store for his seed: "I will increase your numbers greatly [*m'od*]" was the promise. We can turn to the Psalms again: the writer of Psalm 119 goes to great lengths to express his love for God's words. How much does he love those words? "So much [*m'od*]" (Psalm 119:167).

The word *m'od*, therefore, conveys a sense of "muchness, abundance, force" (Brown, Driver and Briggs 547).

The Talmud notes the similarity of *m'od* to two other words: *middah* (measure) and *modeh* (thanks) (*Ber.* 54a). This can throw light on the meaning of "You shall love the Lord your God with all your *m'od*." Such love, it suggests, is a response of gratitude according to the measure of what God has given us.

Not surprisingly, the rabbis have interpreted this command to mean that we should love him very, very much indeed. Two modern writers interpret this in slightly different ways. Lamm suggests that we are to love him with all our "very-ness," and that means all that we have in the way of power and possessions (Lamm, 142). Donin points out that such a total love must be unconditional, whether life is easy or hard, in days of both blessing and persecution (Donin, 150).

Possessions

The most usual interpretation of this command is, however, that we are to love God with all our possessions, all our resources. This can be both a positive and a negative command. On the positive side, The Hasidic view has been that *Ahavat HaShem* should so fill us that it actually transforms our possessions into something of worth and beauty. According to the Besht, love of a possession can be sublimated and so can augment our love for God. "When you fall in love with an earthly pleasure, consider that the power of love was vouchsafed unto you for the purpose of loving God, not for unworthy things. Then you will find it easy to serve God with the love awakened in your heart" (Newman 137).

Hirsch, writing in 19th century Europe, had more of an orthodox theology than a mystical theology. He saw things in terms of *doing*. Possessions, he said, are to be a means to loving God with our service:

> In the life which has been lent to you, in your physical powers, your health and bodily fitness, in the resources which you have acquired, in the whole endowment which God has given you in

the material world—money, business, honour, influence, friends, family—that in all of these you may see only the means and instruments for accomplishing that which God in his law has meant to be accomplished...your life and your possessions will be dedicated to this one effort [loving God]. (Hirsch, 27)

Telushkin, in our own day, feels that the command to love God with all our possessions means that we must be generous with them. This thought leads him to the more demanding interpretation of the command. Loving God with all our might, or resources, means loving him with all our possessions. It is an instruction to be generous with what God has given us, and to be willing to lose everything if he asks it of us (Telushkin, 359). We are to dedicate everything we have to the service of God. If it is of no use to God, we should cast it away—it is of no value. Nothing is worth compromising our faithfulness to God. Everything that is most dear to us is of less value than God's commands. Rather than break the least of these, said Hirsch, we should abandon everything, without hesitation (Hirsch, 28).

Are we, then, to give up all our material possessions? This has been the subject of rabbinical debate. Some have said that one only needs do so in order to avoid the three most serious categories of sin: murder, idolatry and certain sexual sins. Others have felt that this interpretation does not go far enough.

The Hasidic view would seem to be more penetrating. Rabbi Achneur Zalman, a Hasidic master, expressed it like this:

We cannot command our feelings; it is difficult to summon up the emotion of love. What we can do, however, is remove any impediment within us; anything in our lives that might hinder us from loving God with our whole being. Possessions might become such an impediment, in which case we are better without them. The love of God is potentially within all Isra'el. It is up to us to keep the channel of this love unblocked. (Lamm, 96)

The Talmudist Rabbi Meir Simha of Dvinsk read a measure of endurance into the command. He felt that the word *m'od* indicates "more," or "extra." Man has an ability, he taught, that animals do not possess, to endure present hardship for the sake of future benefits. We must offer to God this ability to defer present gratification. This means we determine to offer him love even though we may feel no response of love from him at the time. We trust him enough to be confident that ultimately our offering of love will be acknowledged, accepted, and reciprocated (Lamm, 145).

Heart, Being, Resources

How can we sum up this threefold command to love the Lord our God with all our heart, with all our being, and with all our resources?

The Kossover, an 18th century disciple of the Besht, set it in the context of the whole Sh'ma. "Let us swear that with our whole heart, our whole soul and our entire fortune we shall express the Lord's Kingdom and Unity" (Newman, 142).

Philo, the first century c.e. Alexandrian Philosopher, took flight, and needed more words to express his interpretation:

> The wise man should dedicate his sagacity, the eloquent man should devote his excellence of speech...the natural philosopher should offer his physics, the moralist his ethics, the artist and the man of science the arts and sciences they know. So, too, the sailor and the pilot will dedicate their favorable voyage, the husbandman his fruitful harvest, the herdsman the increase of his cattle, the doctor the recovery of his patients, the general his victory in fight, and the statesman or the monarch his rule. All should be offered to the praise of God. (*The Dedicated Life*, Philo Judaeus. Hertz, *A Book of Jewish Thoughts* 289)

We offer him what we can, and what we have. Listen to one of the medieval sweet singers of Isra'el:

> What is it that the heart
> or the tongue can do,
> And what power is there
> In the spirit that is in me?

But I know you are pleased
With the songs that men make,
And so I shall praise you
While the divine soul is in me. (*In the Morning*, Solomon Ibn
Gabirol. Leviant, 180)

Yeshua

If we are thinking about being generous to the point of sacrifice
with all our resources and possessions, Yeshua is the supreme example. Others have given generously, at great cost. Consider, however, that Yeshua had much more to start with, much more to give,
much more to lose. His rightful place is in the glory of heaven, and
his rightful status is majesty. His rightful environment is light and
beauty. His rightful company is with the Father and the angels, and
his rightful due is worship. All this he gave up in order to enter the
human condition and identify with humanity. Sha'ul understood
this so clearly:

> Though he was in the form of God,
> he did not regard equality with God
> something to be possessed by force.
> On the contrary, he emptied himself,
> in that he took the form of a slave
> by becoming like human beings are.

> And when he appeared as a human being,
> he humbled himself still more
> by becoming obedient even to death—
> death on a stake as a criminal! (Phil. 2:6–8)

The purpose of this enormous sacrifice was that he might restore humanity to fellowship with God. He was able to do this because, as Rabbi Meir Simha put it, he could "defer current
gratification." The *B'rit Hadashah* puts it like this: "Yeshua, in ex-
change for obtaining the joy set before him, endured execution on
a stake as a criminal, scorning the shame, and has sat down at the
right hand of the throne of God" (Heb. 12:2).

Yeshua, the human being, was liberal with his gifting. His
teaching gifts, backed up by the miracles, were expended until he
was too exhausted to go on, needing to withdraw temporarily in
order to continue more of the same (Mark 6:45–52). We know

that his healing ministry was equally, if not more, costly. He *felt* the power going out of him when the woman touched his *tzitzit* (Mark 5:30). His compassion had no limits. His magnetic personality and gift for friendship were dedicated only to reconciling people to God and one another; never did he abuse those gifts in order to achieve personal popularity or power. His leadership gifts and much of his teaching were concentrated on preparing a group of not very promising *talmidim* to take up the burden of proclamation after his departure.

The *Talmidim*

We have already thought about Sha'ul: how he gave of his intellectual abilities. He had spent years at the feet of the great Gamaliel. He would have learned to think, to argue, to exercise mental ingenuity. He drew on all this training as he proclaimed, taught, wrote, and agonized over the infant Messianic community. He was also acquainted with Greek culture. This meant that he was able to meet pagan philosophers on their own ground (Acts 17:22–34). As a Roman citizen, he could not be easily dismissed. The final chapters of Acts show how he took advantage of that fact to reach the heart of the Roman Empire with the gospel. Everything he had, and was, he threw at the feet of his beloved Messiah.

There were others. I would like to pick out some of the women, because the men are already well known. Miryam, the mother of Yeshua, gave up her reputation, and risked her marriage prospects, when she said, "I am the servant of ADONAI; may it happen to me as you have said" (Luke 1:38).

There was one who had no reputation or marriage prospects left to sacrifice. She broke an expensive jar of anointing perfume (perhaps a tool of her trade?) over Yeshua. This too was acceptable to him.

When the Lord gave my husband and me the gift of daughters, we considered what names to give them. Names are significant in Jewish culture. What did we hope for with these girls? We chose Susannah (*Shoshanah*) and Joanna (*Yochanah*). Why? These two women were among those who "drew on their own wealth to help him" (Luke 8:3). They used their own resources to minister to

Yeshua and the other disciples. What more did we hope for our daughters than that they should love the Lord their God with all their hearts, all their beings, and all their resources?

For Thought

We can be guilt-tripped over this matter of loving, and serving, the Lord with all our resources. It is easy to see a job that needs doing and think, "I should do that." Many congregations function that way. There is a list of ministries currently in operation, and a list of gaps needing to be filled in order to continue those ministries. When new people come in they are drafted into those gaps. We have people in children's work who have no rapport with youngsters, and women who have teaching gifts arranging flowers and making cakes. I speak with feeling, as one who is overwhelmed with flowers and mediocre on the cooking front. Ask my children! Yet I was well into middle age before I felt comfortable with myself in church life. Congregations, as well as individuals, can be wasteful of God-given resources.

How can we though, as individuals, love the Lord our God with all our resources? This command requires action, not feelings. Surely, at the heart of the believer's life there needs to be an old-fashioned concept-surrender. My spiritual mother once asked me, "Irene, what do you want?" I remember answering, "I want to be what He wants me to be, and do what He wants me to do." I believe now, many years later, that those are the words God wants to hear. He knows we will fall, make mistakes. These words however, spoken whole-heartedly, will turn us into pliable clay that he can transform into absolutely anything.

This love in action is unconditional, as Donin suggests. It is not to be held in abeyance while some particular situation gets resolved-it dictates that resolution. It does not wither and die because the feeling has gone out of worship and God does not seem to care-it hangs on in there, believing that God is faithful to his promises and will never forsake us. It does not falter because God might ask something of us that we really do not want to give-it trusts that even if he asks that most precious thing, it is because he loves us and wants what is ultimately best for us.

The Hasidim felt the urgency of relinquishing all possessions that might impede their love of God. How much more should we, who are conscious of the price paid for our redemption in Yeshua! Philo wanted to offer all to God's praise. How can we do less? The Kossover sought to offer everything he had so that it might express God's kingdom and unity. Surely my heart's desire is that I may express, in the totality of my life, the beauty, the integrity, the uniqueness of my Messiah and Savior, Yeshua.

A Prayer

Lord, sometimes I feel that I am operating at half-capacity. Then at other times I seem to be over-loaded and running on dry. I really do want to lay at your feet all my resources. Help me to know what those resources are, to recognize my own gifting, to know myself.

Lord I know that nothing I have is mine by right. I want to lay at your feet all my possessions, all my gifts. They come to me because you are gracious, not because I am deserving. I do not need them; I only need you. I am your servant. Do with me as you will. I just want to be what you want me to be, and do what you want me to do.

Blessed are you, O Lord our God, King of the universe, who has blessed us with all manner of gifts to use in your service, for your glory.

A Call
To Do

CHAPTER 11

Love Your Neighbor As Yourself

אַהַבְתָּ לְרֵעֲךָ כָּמוֹךָ

Ahavta l're'acha kamecha

The world endures because of three activities: Torah study, worship of God, and deeds of lovingkindness (*Av.* 1:2).

"This is what the Holy One said to Israel: My children, what do I seek from you? I seek no more than that you love one another and honor one another" (Telushkin 177, citing a 10th century saying).

"Among the greatest commandments He gave us is the law of loving our neighbour" (Epstein 63).

The *mitzvah* of loving our neighbor is not part of the Sh'ma, though it is of course biblical: "Love your neighbor as yourself; I am ADONAI" (Lev. 19:18). I have inserted it here for two reasons. Firstly, it is totally in tune with Jewish tradition and Jewish ethics to see love of God as being inseparable from the way we treat other people. Secondly, The Jewish Messiah himself presented the two together as the summing up of "All of the Torah and the Prophets" (Matt. 22: 36–40).

One God—One Humanity

The call to love one's neighbor is relevant in the context of the Sh'ma because it relates to the oneness of God. The prophet Mal'achi (Malachi) taught: "Don't we all have the same father? Didn't one God create us all?" (Mal. 2:10). The prophet's immediate concern may have been for relationships within the people of

Isra'el, but his words are a basis for the Jewish belief in the brotherhood of all mankind. If we believe that the creator God is One, then it follows that all created people are children of the same Father—brothers and sisters to each other. All carry the image of the One God. The term One God implies one humanity. One humanity demands the brotherhood of all.

Love of God—Love of Neighbor

The two loves are inseparable. One can view this teaching in two ways. Realizing that mankind as a race is not naturally altruistic, Epstein pointed out that without the undergirding of our love for God, it is not possible truly to love other people. Conversely, Plaut quotes a Hasidic source observing that of the three times the Torah asks us to love, two are in Leviticus (19: 18, 34) and concern loving human beings. Only one, in Deuteronomy (6:5), concerns loving God. This, he says, indicates that loving people comes first. Only after we have learned to love people can we hope to achieve love of God (Plaut, 1375).

Whichever interpretation we favor, it is clear that if we love God wholeheartedly we shall also love our fellow human beings. It is our love of people that demonstrates our love of God; there cannot be the one without the other. That is the plain teaching in every Jewish tradition. Epstein, the orthodox teacher, noted that the command includes the words, "I am ADONAI." The Hasidic Rabbi Israel Isaac of Alexander said this inclusion indicates that we are to include God in the compact of loving our neighbor (Newman, 224).

What is This Love?

Love of one's neighbor has both a positive and a negative aspect. We are to do to others as we would wish them to do to us. Conversely, we must not do to others what we do not wish them to do to us. The Talmud records that the great Rabbi Hillel, who was a near contemporary of Yeshua, was once asked to teach the whole

Torah while the questioner stood on one leg. Apparently he responded: "What is hateful to you, do not to your neighbor. That is the whole Torah, while the rest is commentary thereof, go and learn it" (*Shab.* 31a).

The *mitzvah* goes beyond mere duty. Justice requires us to do no harm to others. Righteousness is more demanding; it requires us to do what is good to others. Love motivates us to *want* to do treat other people well. Not only doing, but also caring, is involved; not only physical, but also social needs are to be our concern. Our fellow man's honor is to be as precious to us as our own.

Love takes us beyond what is easy, convenient. There is a particular act of love known as *Li-fenim mi-shurath ha-din* (withdrawing from the line). This means that we concede something that is rightfully ours, in favor of someone whose need is greater. We are to be prepared to help others even if the cost is sacrificial.

Tzedakah (Righteousness)

There are certain things that it is our duty to do as a part of loving our neighbor. We have to give alms to the poor; provide for the aged, the sick, and the orphaned; help the foreigner. Helping the poor is more than just forking out money. It involves taking the trouble to get them to the place where they can support themselves. We must provide education for the children of the poor. We should encourage the needy, not humiliating them. We should raise up and rehabilitate those who have fallen. All this is tzedakah, deeds of righteousness. God will bless us as we are a blessing to those around us (Deuteronomy 15:7–11.)

Gemilut Hasadim (Acts of Love)

One may perform *tzedakot* entirely out of a sense of duty. *Gemilut Hasadim* requires something more: we must perform the duty in a spirit of love and compassion. To visit the sick may be a duty, to be done as a matter of form. Only if we do it with the object of ameliorating the distress of the bereaved will the duty be an act of love. It is a Jewish axiom that we fail not to be with them that weep, and mourn with them that mourn.

Other *Gemilut Hasadim* include providing a dowry for the bride, helping to make the wedding a happy occasion, assisting in setting up the new home. It is of the utmost importance to attend a funeral, accompanying the dead to the grave. This is regarded as an act of pure love, because it is the only *mitzvah* where the recipient can never reciprocate! Peacemaking is also in this category. It is not enough to avoid quarrels oneself. One must endeavor, wherever possible, to establish peace and goodwill between others. One must always try to look for the best in others. It is so easy to pick out other people's worst traits. "A man filled with love ...will *think* kindly of others...will be courteous and patient...will readily forgive and forget the offence" (Epstein, 51).

Rabbi Moses Leib of Sassov, Sassover a Hasidic Rabbi, taught that love involves a degree of sensitivity, of understanding what brings pain to another (Newman, 221). Martin Buber, the twentieth century philosopher, took this idea even further. He saw neighborly love as more than deeds. The deeds have to stem from a personal empathy with the suffering of another, a sharing of his burden (Telushkin, 176). We not only *know* our neighbor's pains and joys. We *feel* them. We *bear* them. We *participate* in them.

Hirsch sums up the concept: "In *gemilut chasadim* you place on God's sacred altar all the best and noblest you have—your judgment, your word, your strength, your deeds, your entire personality—for the good of your brethren" (Hirsch, 432).

The Sixth Word

The commandment to love one's neighbor is an extension of the sixth Word given on Sinai: "Do not murder" (Exod. 20:13). We must not take a life by violent means; neither may we doing anything that could undermine the health, the peace, or the well-being of another person. Furthermore, we may not sin against another by failing to do anything in our power to save them from danger. Maimonides taught that the purpose of the laws of Torah was not just negative—to forbid certain actions—but positive. They are "to bring mercy, lovingkindness and peace upon the world" (*Mishneh* Torah 2:3).

Who is My Neighbor?

In Jewish tradition, the term 'neighbor' does not apply to all people indiscriminately. Epstein defined neighbors as people who behave decently towards society. They need not be our next-door neighbors. They need not be close to us in blood or even in race or religion. As fellow human beings they are entitled to our respect and our love (Epstein, 51–53).

The command encompasses close relationships—between parents and children, between friends, between husband and wife, within the Jewish community, and business relationships. It excludes, however, those who are anti-social—the criminally minded, the cruel, the dishonest. The expression "Hate the sin, love the sinner" has limits in Jewish eyes. A post-Holocaust writer has pointed out that "those who love Hitler are less likely to fight him than those who hate him" (Dennis Prager, quoted by Telushkin, 195).

The stranger in the midst, however, is most definitely included in this command. Torah is quite clear: "If a foreigner stays with you in your land, do not do him wrong. Rather, treat the foreigner staying with you like the native-born among you—you are to love him as yourself, for you were foreigners in the land of Egypt; I am ADONAI your God" (Lev. 19:33–34). The term "foreigner" applies to a visitor, a refugee, one who has come to you in need. Even if such a person becomes a burden, you must shoulder that burden with brotherly love. "The same Torah and standard of judgment will apply to both you and the foreigner living with you" (Num. 15:16).

We do not have to like our neighbors; we do not have to *feel* loving toward them. It is what we *do* that matters. Jewish duty is to stand by the needy, and to support and help the losers we encounter along life's way. As the prophet Mikhah directed: "You have already been told what is good, what ADONAI demands of you—no more than to act justly, love grace and walk in purity with your God" (Mic. 6:8).

Yeshua

Yeshua, tell us please. Who exactly is my neighbor? (Luke 10:25–37).

My neighbor is the person in my path, who has a need that I am able to meet. I am his neighbor if I overcome my personal and racial prejudices about him; if I see him as a fellow human being not as a category; if I put myself at a disadvantage, even at risk, on his behalf. I am her neighbor if I overcome my personal and racial prejudices about her; if I see her as a fellow human being not as a category; if I put myself at a disadvantage, even at risk, on her behalf.

Yeshua is reiterating sound, traditional, Jewish teaching here. He is also interpreting that teaching, applying it to the here and now. He is challenging current prejudices in the light of the present situation. I wonder how he would have expressed the parable now, in the early 21ˢᵗ century?

Yeshua longed to see his followers showing love one to another. He prayed earnestly that this would happen. He asked that the unity of God would be reflected in the unity of the community (John 17:21). He also taught that true love of him would be seen in acts of love shown to the needy (Matt. 25:34–40). We can see, however, that the parable of the Good Samaritan holds a more demanding challenge. It takes his followers out of the comfort zone, so to speak. It demands that Yeshua's followers reach out in neighborly love beyond the boundaries of community, of common interests and purpose.

What is more revolutionary in the context of this command, however, is not so much his teaching as his actions. He had taught that God's love for people was such that he gave his only Son that they might not die but live (John 3:16). That is a huge picture of love. Perhaps we cannot understand it. We can, however, accept it because it speaks of mankind in general terms. It is very much harder to take on board the love he lived out on the Cross, in a specific situation, for a specific group of people who were treating him with unbelievable cruelty:

> "Father, forgive them; they don't understand what they are doing" (Luke 23:34).

Look at all the requirements of neighborly love. See them here pinpointed, at this one moment in time. Truly this man acted justly, loved grace, and walked in purity with God. Truly this man loved his neighbor. He loved the man on the cross next to his, though whatever did they have in common? He loved those who were torturing him and mocking him, though they showed him nothing but contempt.

Messianic Teaching

Yeshua's teaching on love and a life of love had a tremendous impact on his early followers. Ya'akov (James) rated *gemilut hasadim* high as a priority in the community (James 1:27). People in need were to be treated with respect, given dignity (2:5–9). Faith without *tzedakah* is meaningless, without value (2:20).

Sha'ul had a broad interpretation of "neighbor." He told the Galatian messianic community to stop snapping at one another's' heels. "The whole of the Torah is summed up in this one sentence: 'Love your neighbor as yourself'" (Gal. 5:14). In the wider picture, however, his teaching was that your neighbor is your "fellow human being" (Rom. 13:8), and you owe him/her love. Most of the Ten Words, said Sha'ul, are about love of neighbor (Gal. 5:14). Fulfill those, and you have fulfilled Torah.

Ya'akov connected neighborly love with faith, and Sha'ul with obedience to Torah. It fell to John to make the link with God's love for us and ours for him. Speaking specifically about love within the community, he taught:

> We ourselves love now because he loved us first. If anyone says, "I love God," and hates his brother, he is a liar. For if a person does not love his brother, whom he has seen, then he cannot love God, whom he has not seen. Yes, this is the command we have from him: whoever loves God must love his brother too (1 John 4:19–21).

For Thought

Those who follow Yeshua the Messiah have to face the fact that failure in the matter of neighborly love is the biggest scar across the history of "Christianity." Too often concepts like 'faith' and 'truth' have been stripped of soul and, defaced into ugliness, set above love. The Master rated love of one's neighbor as the *mitzvah* second only to love of God. How dare the Church try to separate faith and truth from love!

We must deplore the actions of the historic "Church." Of course we must. Let us, however, look to ourselves as present-day believers. Where is that oneness that Yeshua saw to be the reflection of God's oneness? Where is it in the wider Messianic Community? Where is it in our congregations? Why is it that we suffer more pain within the fellowship than we do in the world outside? See this command set in its context: "Don't...bear a grudge against any of your people; rather, love your neighbor as yourself; I am ADONAI" (Lev. 19:18). I hear Yeshua, broken-hearted and broken-voiced, yearning still: "Oh that they might be one, as you and I are one. Then the world will see..."

A Prayer

Avinu Malkheynu, our Father our King, our fathers and we seem to be utterly incapable of fulfilling the command to love our neighbor. Yet you ask it of us, so it must be possible, in the power of your Holy Spirit. Please enable me to love the needy, and my brothers and sisters in Messiah (all of them!).

I find it hard even to love myself, though I know that you love me. I find it hard to love some people, but I know that you love them.

I think that some people find it hard to love me. Show me, Father, what to do now, in my present situation, to promote love and oneness in my family, my congregation, and my community. Never let me make it hard for someone else to love you through me.

Blessed are you, O Lord my God, King of the Universe, who has loved me with an everlasting love, and requires me to reflect that love to others.

CHAPTER 12

On Your Heart

תֵּל כּשׁשׁל

Al l'vav'cha

"These words, which I am ordering you today, are to be on your heart" (Deut. 6:6).

These Words

There has been much discussion about what is meant by the term "these words." Does it mean the words of the Sh'ma up to this point? Is it the whole of the Sh'ma? Does it embrace Torah in its entirety? It seems that in the early days the talmudic sages understood it to mean the whole of the Sh'ma. Later, the Rabbis taught that all of Torah was indicated.

There are yet other views. Some have said "these words" are those verses placed in the tefillin. That would be Exod. 13:1–10, 11–16; Deut. 6:4–9, 13–21. Hertz believed them to be just verses four and five of Deuteronomy chapter six (Hertz, *Deuteronomy* 86).

Today

The inclusion of the word "today," taught Rashi, means that the words should always be fresh, each day, never appearing stale, or out-of-date (Rashi, *Deuteronomy* 37). This means that one must recite the Sh'ma with proper attention, with kavannah (*Ber.* 13b). It would be all too easy to slip into a mindless repetition of the words. One must speak them fluently, clearly, and with conviction, so that others can hear and understand.

Torah

Through the insecurity and rootlessness of the Diaspora since the destruction of the Temple, Jewish people have found their security in Torah. That may be why the Rabbis have interpreted "these words" to mean the whole of Torah.

Torah is Judaism's greatest treasure. Heine, in 1830, described generations of Jewish people totally absorbed in the study of the "Book of Books" (Hertz. *A Book of Jewish Thoughts* 57). Israel Zangwill, writing in 1895, declared that compared with the Bible all other literature is as light as air—of little account (Hertz, *A Book of Jewish Thoughts* 59). Torah has been Judaism's precious gift to the world. Schechter, in 1903, wrote that it has been Isra'el's sole "*raison d'etre*." The Jewish people have guarded it with their lives, remaining faithful to the death, in the face of a hostile world (Hertz, *A Book of Jewish Thoughts* 60).

Torah and the Human Heart

We have seen that the human heart is considered to be the source of personality and character. It is vital to subject that character to beneficial influences at source, and Torah is the best of all possible influences. Therefore we must inscribe the words of Torah on our hearts, in order that those words may be an integral part of our being.

There is a tacit acknowledgment that the heart has a bias to evil. As the prophet Yirmeyahu said: "The heart is more deceitful than anything else and mortally sick" (Jer. 17:9). This makes it all the more vital that God's words be placed upon our hearts, so that their influence may be decisive in the way we conduct our lives. That is the only way to counteract the tendency to deceitfulness and wickedness. The human heart is in desperate need of Torah.

Hertz was among those who have been less willing to talk about the natural evil of the human heart. He referred to Yirmeyahu's New Covenant prophecy (Jer. 31:32–33), seeing the heart as "a tablet on which these Divine words shall be inscribed" (Hertz, Deuteronomy 86). We have a responsibility to expose ourselves to Torah, so that God can inscribe its words on our hearts.

In the Sh'ma, this direction immediately follows the command to love God with all one's heart, being and resources. Is there any relationship between loving God with all one's heart and having these words upon one's heart? Indeed there is. It is by contemplating Torah that one comes to a realization of the greatness and awesomeness of God. That is the surest way to invite God's love to come and fill our hearts (Lamm, 153. quoting the *Hinuch*, a medieval work on the 613 Commandments).

There is also a connection between Torah and love of one's neighbor. The Talmud teaches that the world stands on three things: Torah, *avodah* (worship), and *gemilut hasadim* (*Av.* 1:2). Judaism is holistic. One cannot grow in one area of life while ignoring another. Torah study and its practical application go side by side. Love and worship of God must always accompany deeds of loving kindness.

"On," not "In"

My mother-in-law used to say that Judaism is essentially realistic. It does not expect or ask of people more that they can perform. The Rabbis have had this in mind in commenting on the word "on" in this instruction. For most ordinary people the penetration of the divine word *into* the heart is an impossibility. Therefore Torah, given to ordinary people, does not ask it. The most we are capable of is to place those words *upon* our hearts. The Torah meets us where we are and does not ask the impossible. It encourages us to do better. Realizing that "in the heart" is an impossibility, God will accept "on the heart." After all, even that is an achievement!

For every realist, however, there is also an optimist. Lamm quotes Rabbi Menahem Mendel of Kotzk, whose words may encourage those condemned to teach pupils who are apparently obtuse and non-receptive:

> Even if you feel that your heart is shut tight and words of Torah do not penetrate it—because you are weary or inattentive or preoccupied or simply dull—do not despair.... Just let the words pile up *upon* your heart. Be confident that in due time your heart will open up, and when it does, inspiration will come. Then, all that has been gathered in, lying patiently *upon* your heart, will tumble *into* your newly opened heart. (Lamm, 152)

The Study of Torah

Another interpretation of this direction is that it refers to Torah study. The relationship between study and love is a recurring theme in rabbinical Judaism. It is through such study, said Rashi, that we shall learn to recognize and know the Holy One, and cleave to his ways (Rashi, *Deuteronomy* 37).

There is a belief that such study needs to be intensive. Donin points to the sequence of petitions in the fifth blessing of the *Amidah* (Standing Prayer). It begins with "Return us to Thy Torah"; then moves on to "Draw us near to worship Thee." Finally we pray, "Lead us back in full repentance." Torah study has to be the starting point in developing any relationship with the Almighty. (Donin, 150).

Maimonides took a different view. He taught that one can know and love God better through the contemplation of Creation and nature as well as in Torah. These are God's works, and he reveals himself in them. Maimonides saw godly education as being far broader that just Torah study.

These two views could seem to be in opposition. There can, however, be a reconciliation. A contemplation of nature leads us to appreciate God as Creator. However, it tells us little about his character, personality, or how he chooses to relate to humanity. For that we need to study Torah. This is the kind of study that will enhance and strengthen our love for God.

Torah study is not to be an end in itself; that would be sterile. It must always lead to action—to obedience—to a disciplined and God-fearing life. The belief is that when God comes to assess my life, he will first demand why I have not studied. Then he will ask why I have not performed that which I studied. The Rabbinical tradition is that: "If a man learns the words of the Torah, he has fulfilled one command; if he learns and guards them, he has fulfilled two; if he learns and guards and does them, there is no one greater than he" (Montefiore, 174).

Kavanah

This kind of intensive, soul-searching study requires a whole-hearted, devoted approach; a purely academic interest will not do.

The Hasidic teachers have been most particular about this. The Besht was particularly scathing about purely academic scholars; to him, study for the sake of scholarship was an abomination. Torah study should be an expression of the heart's devotion to God (Newman, 456). If God's words are truly on our hearts, there will be inner transformation that will affect the whole of life. The Bratzlaver, great grandson of the Besht, taught that "He who works untiringly on the study of Torah until he understands it, heals his soul, and raises it to its Source, thereby increasing God's glory" (Newman, 462).

Yeshua and *Tanakh*

Yeshua had the Scriptures on his heart, in his mind, and at his fingertips. In the story of the temptations, we see him using them as a shield against Satan's wiles (Matt. 4:1–10). He was following the Psalmist's example: "I treasure your word in my heart, so that I won't sin against you" (Ps. 119:11).

He used that Word to teach about his Messianic identity in the synagogue at Nazareth (Luke 4: 16–21), and again as he wept over Jerusalem: "For I tell you, from now on, you will not see me again until you say, 'Blessed is he who comes in the name of ADONAI'" (Matt. 23:39). Those words were a quotation from Psalm 118, associated with the coming of the expected Messiah. He quoted Isaiah again when Yochanan the Immerser (John the Baptist) sent to ask if he was indeed the expected one (Luke 7:20–23).

When the Torah expert thought to test him, Yeshua, in true Jewish manner, was quick to field the question with a counter-question: "What is written in the Torah? How do you read it?" (Luke 10:26). The clear implication of these words is: "Torah has the authoritative answer."

He was able to justify his actions from *Tanakh* when he cleansed the Temple (Luke 19:45–46). When the Torah-teachers thought to confound him with a question, he was able to confound them with an even harder one concerning messianic prophecy (Luke 20:41–44). He constantly enhanced his teaching with references to *Tanakh* (e.g. Matt. 9:13; 13:14–15; 19:18–22; 21:42).

Finally, it was words of Scripture that came to his mind as he hung, dying, on that Cross: "*Eli! Eli! L'mah sh'vaktani?* (My God! My God! Why have you abandoned me?)" (Ps. 22:1(2)). Then again, at the end, he cried: "Into your hands I commit my spirit" (Ps. 31:5(6)). Only the Bible-soaked person will quote *Tanakh* in such extremity!

The Early *Talmidim*

It is not surprising that, with the example of Yeshua before them, the early leaders of the messianic community were steeped in the words of *Tanakh*. They lived by them and taught from them, and they made sure that the gentile believers absorbed them. We see them constantly referred to in all the New Covenant writings.

Kefa (Peter) used them on that festival of *Shavu'ot* (Pentecost) when the Holy Spirit descended in power, and many turned to God in repentance and belief (Acts 2).

Stephen's reasoned defense was full of scripture (Acts 7). It was Philip's understanding of *Tanakh* that enabled him to satisfy the questioning heart of the Ethiopian eunuch (Acts 8:26–35).

Sha'ul's early sermon at Antioch was liberally sprinkled with scriptural quotations (Acts 13:16–31). Years later, his advice to the younger Timothy was that *Tanakh* is able impart a wisdom that may lead to faith in Yeshua the Messiah. That is because "All Scripture is God-breathed and is valuable for teaching the truth, convicting of sin, correcting faults and training in right living" (2 Tim. 3:15–16).

For Thought

"I will put my Torah within them and write it on their hearts" (Jer. 31:33(32)). These words from the New Covenant promise in Jeremiah were primarily addressed to Isra'el. Yeshua claimed to be the fulfillment of that New Covenant at his last *Pesach Seder*. As he shared the third cup—the Cup of Redemption—he described it as "my blood, which ratifies the New Covenant...shed on behalf of many, so that they may have their sins forgiven" (Matt. 26:28). By implication he was referring back to the prophecy of Jeremiah, teaching them that the time had now come for Torah to be embedded within his followers, and written on their hearts. This is a common rabbinical device: words are not actually spoken but they are clearly understood by everyone present.

It is possible for us, as followers of Yeshua, to have Torah written on our hearts and placed within our beings. This will not happen by our own efforts. God promises to do it. God's promises, however, need our cooperation and our openness. If I truly want him to write his Torah on my heart I will read and study it. If I sincerely long to have his Torah *within* me, I will study it with the intention of letting it change my life. This will be a life-long discipline and joy.

Whom do we turn to for authority? A common criticism of Judaism is that authority is vested in tradition rather than in the Bible. Protestant Christians make the same judgment concerning Roman Catholics, but Protestants can be just as guilty. How often we hear the words, "We've always done it this way"! I am reminded of Yeshua's words to the *talmidim*. He had asked them what people were saying about him. Some were saying this and some that. "But you," Yeshua responded, "who do you say I am?" (Matt. 16:15). Perhaps we should look to ourselves, and not be so concerned with the failings of others? Maybe Yeshua asks each one of us, "Where is your authority?" Is our authority the Bible, or is it what this or that great speaker says *about* the Bible?

Yeshua had the Scriptures at his fingertips, but he never used them as a stick with which to beat people. His evangelism did not consist of punching out a bunch of proof-texts in order to prove other people wrong! They were his guide, his direction, and they were his tool for defeating temptation. They were the foundation for his teaching ministry. They were his device for making people think about his own identity. They were his comfort and assurance in distress. What are they to us?

A Prayer

Lord, I am so grateful that you have given me your Word. It has indeed been a light to my path and a lamp to my feet when the way ahead has sometimes been dark. Maybe a time will come when I am not free to read it, or my eyes fail so that I can no longer see the print. Help me now to hide it away in my heart so that no one will be able to take it from me. Your words are gold and silver to me; they are sweeter than honey, more pleasant than wine.

Blessed are you, O Lord our God, King of the universe, who has graciously given us your written Word, and who undertakes to write that Word in our hearts.

CHAPTER 13

Teach Them Carefully To Your Children

שַׁנַּנְתָּם לְבָנֶיךָ

Shinan'tam l'banecha

"The place where a child's soul breathes is holy ground"
(Hirsch, 413).

Jewish people have always taken this injunction very seriously. As soon as a child can speak, he learns to recite the Sh'ma. When he is old enough to read, he receives his first Hebrew lesson. The sages taught that boys should begin to study the Scriptures at the age of five (*Av.* 5:24). As he matures, he is taught Torahboth as a reading primer and for moral training. At ten years he studies Mishnah. By the time he comes to his b*ar mitzvah* (religious coming-of-age), at the age of thirteen, he is expected to be quite a skilled Hebrew reader. He needs to be able to master the cantillation (the phrasing and intoning for reading Torah in the synagogue). He will also have to give a brief exposition of his portion at the meal after the service on his big day.

It is the responsibility of the father to teach his child. He may delegate this responsibility to someone more learned, but in many circles this is considered to be a second-best arrangement. My husband regretted all his life that his father had to employ another rabbi to prepare him for his b*ar mitzvah*, because he himself was serving as a chaplain in the army during World War I.

This direction is, however, more than a family matter. The nation of Isra'el is responsible for the nation's children, and that responsibility includes education. Most synagogues have organized classes for teaching religion and Hebrew to the children of members. There is an early 13th century Jewish Code of Education in England, which stipulates that each teacher shall not take more than ten students.

Rashi defined "children" as "disciples." He cited 2 Kings 2:3, where the Hebrew speaks of the guild of prophets as *b'nei haneviim* (sons of the prophets). Likewise, disciples would address their teacher as "father" (2 Kings 2:12).

In the past, men expected to continue their studies in Torah and Talmud all their life. Indeed, not until the age of fifteen did one even begin to study *Talmud* (*Av.* 5:24). This is not the case in our own times, however. Many families regard the *bar mitzvah* as a purely social occasion—a sort of milestone along life's way. Afterwards, synagogue attendance may dwindle. Learning and religious practice are not given the high priority they once were.

The *Hasidim* believed that there was a connection between "These words shall be upon your heart" and "You shall teach them diligently to your children." They reasoned that only as "these words" come out of one's heart will they truly have any impact for good on the lives of one's children. The aim of the teaching is not to increase knowledge in the child. It is that he may know God, know Isra'el's place in the world, and know his own place within Isra'el.

Girls?

In ancient times, it seems that the normal practice was to educate girls as well as boys. In later centuries the rabbis became increasingly unwilling to do this. The Talmud seems to present a mixed message on this subject. Here are two sayings: "A man is under the obligation to teach his daughter Torah" (*Sot.* 20a); "Whoever teaches his daughter Torah teaches her obscenity" (*Sot.* 20a). In the same passage, we find "the female Pharisee" included among those who are "destroyers of the world." In the same tractate, a rabbi is quoted as saying that it would be better to burn the words of Torah than to teach them to women! (Sot. 19a). Cohen, writing in *Everyman's Talmud*, seems to be uncomfortable with the concept of religious education for girls (Cohen, 189).

Why did this happen? Certainly there was a view that sexual morality in the reigning Greek and then Roman society was lax. This may have led to a strict separation of the sexes, and the confining of girls to the domestic sphere.

Today, most synagogues teach the girls as well as the boys. Many quite orthodox families prepare their daughters for *bat mitzvah*. This is a fairly recent development. The British Chief Rabbi of only a century ago saw nothing wrong in the inequitable education of boys and girls:

> In ancient times, the Mishnah speaks of the Scripture instruction of sons and daughters as the normal practice.... If in later centuries the standard of education for Jewish girls was immeasurably lower than it was in the case of boys, it did not much matter; as, in the sheltered life of the old ghetto, Jewish woman remained unharmed by this narrow educational ideal. (Hertz, *Deuteronomy* 151–52)

Teach carefully

Some translations use the word "diligently" here. Lamm points out that the root meaning of *"shinan'tam"* is "sharp, acute" (Lamm, 157). Hertz even renders the expression "prick them in" (Hertz, *Deuteronomy* 86). Why do people tattoo a loved one's name on their bodies? It is as a demonstration that they do not want to forget, and they will not forget! We should so teach our children that God's words remain on their hearts all their lives. More than that, we have a responsibility to introduce them to Torah in such a way that they will discover the joys of learning. Good teachers have fulfilled their responsibility if their charges continue to delight in Torah study as adults. Our task is to enlighten minds, enrich memories, and inspire hearts.

Donin sees the meaning as "review it again and again" (Donin, 151). The important thing is that children hear and repeat the words of Torah so often that those words become an indelible part of their being. There is a place here for learning by rote, though not without an understanding of the meaning of the words so learned. It is important that the words of Torah become so familiar that the child will develop a clear picture of what it means to be a Jew. He will know how to conduct himself in any situation, how to answer any question. Rashi believed that the words of Torah should be so familiar to us that we are ready to answer absolutely any question about them, without hesitation (Rashi, *Deuteronomy* 37). The Talmud lays a burden of responsibility on the teacher here. He has to be diligent in his task so that he understands the meaning of Torah, and is able to pass that meaning on to his pupils (*Kidd.* 30a).

Judaism is always realistic, however. The Talmud recognizes that one cannot make a silk purse out of a sow's ear! We read that there are four classes of pupils: A sponge, a funnel, a strainer, and a sieve. A sponge sucks up everything. A funnel lets it in at one end and out at the other. A strainer lets the wine pass out and retains the less. A sieve lets out the bran and retains the fine flour (*Av.* 5:18).

The Importance of Education

Telushkin sees this direction as the ultimate source of Jewish people's age-old respect for education (Telushkin, 359). Education has always been at the top of the agenda. There has been a consciousness that the book of Proverbs speaks true when it says, "Train a child in the way he [should] go; and, even when old, he will not swerve from it" (Prov. 22:6). The Talmud reinforces this tradition, going so far as to say that "We may not suspend the instruction of children even for the rebuilding of the Temple" (*Shab.* 119b).

We all know that it was easier to acquire new knowledge when we were young. So much clutter has accumulated in our minds with the passing of the years and, let's face it, we are not as sharp as we used to be! The Talmud recognizes this, telling us that learning as a child is like ink written on clean paper (*Av.* 4:25). What one learns in youth has a better chance of remaining in the mind and taking root in the heart.

Not to educate a child, therefore, is a serious failure in parenting. The respected twentieth century thinker, Rabbi Moshe Soloveitchik, even saw it as a form of idolatry (Lamm, 158). We deprive the child of the right start in life, with God at the center. This ignorance leaves him unprotected against the hazards and temptations to come.

Education is not, though, to be an end in itself, a closed circuit. It is an equipping for the business of life. Some would argue that this has not always been the case. Here is a pungent comment on Jewish religious education by Dennis Prager:

> In order for a caterpillar to become a beautiful butterfly taking its beauty out into the world, it must first spend time in a cocoon. In order for a Jew to become a beautiful Jew taking his or her beauty into the world, he or she too must first spend time in a cocoon. Unfortunately, most non-Orthodox Jews don't believe in the cocoon, and most Orthodox Jews don't believe in flying into the world. (Telushkin, 617)

Early Days

The Talmud encourages an early start: at five years the child is fit to be taught to read the Bible (*Av.* 5:21). Long before that, however, children learn to say the Sh'ma, and to repeat some prayers and Bible passages in Hebrew. For instance, it is the custom that the youngest present will ask the four questions on Passover night. This is a cherished privilege, and quite small children will achieve it. My own grandson managed them in English the first year he could read. Last year he read the first question in Hebrew and the rest in English. This year he managed them all in Hebrew. Next year the privilege will pass to his younger sibling twins. No doubt we are in for much competition there!

It is the custom in many families to mark the child's sixth birthday with his first Hebrew lesson. Handled properly, this is in an occasion of great excitement. There is a rather crude injunction that recommends stuffing the six-year-old with Torah "like an ox" (*Baba Bathra* 21a). That seems to me, as a teacher, an unfortunate attitude to education, but who am I to judge! We are not stuffing a dead turkey; we are feeding a living person and nurturing his appetite for more. Remember the words "When your children shall ask you"; for some information, the time must be right; the child needs to be ready.

The Role of Parents

The Talmud asks what fathers owe their sons. The answer given is, "To circumcise, redeem [if a first-born], teach him Torah, take a wife for him, and teach him a craft" (*Kidd.* 29a). I think my sons would have had something to say if we had tried to find their wives for them but, apart from that, these are sound directions. If followed, our offspring may have enough sound judgment to choose the right spouses for themselves.

Hirsch felt that the ministry of a father to his son is almost high priestly (Hirsch, 407). Not to have a son, or to lose a son, is a terrible deprivation, because it deprives one of the opportunity to obey the *mitzvah*. One's children are like a bank account for the world to come. The father who rears his children in the Torah is among those who enjoy the fruit of this world while the capital remains for him in the World to Come (*Shab.* 127a).

Alexander Susskind of Grodno suggested that one remember these responsibilities while reciting the Sh'ma. One is thereby claiming the Kingship of God over the generations to come, promising to perpetuate the command to accept "the yoke of Your Kingdom, Divinity, and Lordship" (Plaut, 1369).

The Role of Teachers

Teachers are to be held in high esteem. They are to be honored and obeyed even as are parents. The Rabbis have believed that the teachers of children in Isra'el are the "gardens by the riverside" spoken of in Numbers 24:6. Parents may bring children into the world, but teachers introduce them to the riches of the life to come.

How do we fulfill this requirement in today's climate? In my own country-the United Kingdom-teachers are no longer the respected members of society that they were even half a century ago, even though financially they are a great deal better off. I do not believe we shrug off this matter by writing a large check. We should watch the way we speak to, and about, those who teach our children; likewise we should expect that they conduct themselves in a manner worthy of respect. We should not allow our children to treat teachers with contempt. That discourages good teachers from entering the profession, and only serves to exacerbate the problem.

Schools

The earliest Jewish school system was probably established in the first century B.C.E. In many Jewish communities the Jewish religious schools have been considered as second in importance only to the home. Children have always been regarded as most precious. One can even assess the health of a community by the educational state of its children. There is a story that if an enemy wants to know whether he can conquer a people, he should go and listen at their house of assembly. If he hears the sounds of children learning, he will not be able to destroy the people. If he hears nothing, he will. The lesson drawn from that was that Jerusalem was destroyed only because the children did not attend school but loitered on the streets instead.

Yeshua the Pupil

As was the custom, the young Yeshua received at least a basic religious education. This is not surprising; his father Joseph was, after all, handpicked for the task of raising the Messiah. We know that he had a sound grasp of things from Luke's account of that visit to the Temple at *Pesach* (Passover) when he was twelve years old (Luke 2:41–50). A well-taught student is not only able to spout facts; he also knows what questions to ask. It was Yeshua's ability to ask pertinent questions that seems to have impressed people on this occasion.

We also know that he was not in a hurry to start his public ministry. He submitted himself to his parents, no doubt learning life-skills in the family home. His development and preparation continued right through his twenties.

Yeshua the Teacher

It has always been customary for rabbis to gather around them a band of *talmidim*; Yeshua was no exception. From the beginning of his active ministry he set about calling a select group of "learners," spending a very large proportion of his time with them. They became his extended family (Matt. 12:49). His ministry was short—

only about three years—but his followers were in for the long haul. Their preparation was a top priority for him. He took time to build on the knowledge they already had, gently raising the bar all the time. They may not have understood everything he taught them at the time, but afterwards they surely did. What a teacher!

Yeshua and Family Relationships

There is a Jewish tradition that not to teach a child Torah is to set the child above God in one's affections, and that is idolatry. Yeshua's teaching was similar. No family relationship must come before our relationship with him (Matt. 10:37). The mark of a true disciple is that he/she is God-centered. Likewise, the mark of successful parenting is that one's children too are God-centered.

For Thought

The priority we give to teaching our children God's Word will reveal something about the depth of our love for them. It will also be an indicator of our love for the Lord himself. If we love him, how can we keep silent about him in our own homes?

Many people reading this chapter will be reliving experiences of failure. We can all see where our parents failed us. Many of us can also see where we ourselves have failed as parents. These can be very depressing thoughts. However, God be praised, we serve a forgiving Master. For us older ones, consciousness of our own failures should at least make us a little charitable about the failures of the younger generation of parents.

Parents today need a great deal of support, particularly those who seek to raise their children with godly, Messiah-centered standards. In my country, the whole social ethic is against them. They do not need criticism; they need understanding, and they need friendship. Being a young mother is a lonely and wearing business. I am not too old to remember dreading taking my four children to worship services, and longing for the time when I could start having a proper "quiet time" again.

I have a word here for those who feel their parents failed them. That word is "forgiveness." Your parents also were victims of their genes and their environment. They were fallible, sinful men and women, just as you are. You can ruin your life by holding onto bitterness and resentment—yes, and even hatred—against them. Let it go. Forgive, even as Messiah has forgiven you.

The goal of any teaching must be love. We are to teach our children God's words so that they may know him and, in knowing him, love him.

A Prayer

Lord, sometimes I feel I am trapped in a cycle of failure. I remember how my parents failed me, and I am conscious that I fail my children. This means that I am locked into negative feelings about my family and about myself. Help me please, O my Lord. Release me. Set me free to be the parent my children need me to be.

Thank you, Father, for your skill and patience in teaching me. As you live in me, may I share in those qualities.

Thank you also, Father, for your ready forgiveness. Forgive me now for the sins of bitterness and resentment against my parents, as you plant your forgiveness in my own heart. As I learn to forgive and receive forgiveness, may my love for you grow.

Blessed are you, O Lord our God, King of the universe, who promises that if the Son frees us, we shall be really free. Set us free to know and love you.

CHAPTER 14

Talk About Them

דברת בם

Dibar'ta bam

"You are to talk about them when you sit at home, when you are traveling on the road, when you lie down and when you get up" (Deut. 6:7).

Sit—Walk—Lie—Rise

The general interpretation of this direction is that there is no time when the Torah should not be a part of our lives. The words of God should be our constant preoccupation all through the day, from early till late, wherever we find ourselves, whatever we are doing. A narrower view is that one should recite the Sh'ma constantly, when performing all sorts of mundane activities (*Ber.* 11a).

A Constant Occupation

"Make them [these words] a constant occupation, not something casual" says the Talmud (*Yoma* 19b). Torah is to be our main preoccupation, not something secondary, worthy of only occasional, passing mention. It is the solid core of our lives, not an added extra. Rashi taught that the words of Torah should be the principle topic of all conversation (Rashi, *Deuteronomy* 38).

Another view is that one should not interrupt our Torah study for idle talk. Discussion is acceptable, because that is a valid aspect of study. Not to engage in conversation at all would be to treat people with contempt. Surely this view is an example of the fact that in Judaism there is no separation between the secular and the sacred. All has the potential to be holy—conversation as much as study. The important thing is that in the whole of our lives, but particularly in our talking, we accord Torah primacy of place. That one way of demonstrating our love for God.

This teaching has its basis in Scripture. The book of Proverbs deals with the power of the spoken word. "The speech of the righteous is a fountain of life, but the speech of the wicked is a cover for violence," says Shlomo (Solomon). Our words are the fruit of what we are: "The mouth of the righteous brings forth wisdom." Our words can be a tremendous force for evil, but also for good: "The lips of the righteous feed many" (Prov. 10:11, 31, 21). The prophet Tz'fanyah, looking ahead to a sinless future, specifically mentioned the tongue as well as the general way of life: "The remnant of Isra'el will do no wrong; nor will they speak lies, nor will there be found in their mouths a tongue given over to deceit" (Zeph. 3:13).

When God commissioned Y'hoshua (Joshua) after the death of Moshe, he commanded him: "Be strong, be bold...taking care to follow all the Torah which Moshe my servant ordered you to follow." He then added a further command. "Keep this book of the Torah on your lips, and meditate on it day and night." Here is a man of action being commissioned. One would think God might excuse him from the day and night meditation, the in-depth study, and the biblical conversation. Not at all. This was a military leader who prayed before going into battle: "Lord, I shall not have time to think of you today, but please will you not forget me." Y'hoshua was not to be like that. His military success would depend on his relationship with God, developed and practiced in the school of meditation, study, and the stimulation of godly conversation. The promise was clear: "Then your undertakings will prosper, and you will succeed" (Josh. 1:6–8). The godly life has no specialists. All are general practitioners.

At Home

There are two ways the directions concerning "at home" have been practiced. The literal way is that all conversation is subject to the demands of religion. For example, a group of orthodox friends may have gathered for ordinary social intercourse. When evening approaches it is a matter of course to break off conversation temporarily in order to say afternoon and evening prayers. There is nothing self-conscious about this; it is a part of life.

The wider interpretation is that this direction concerns the way we conduct ourselves in our homes. The head of the household should create an atmosphere of godliness, of serenity and joy. One's bearing in the home at all times should be such as will stimulate household members towards godliness and right living.

Corporate Study

The Mishnah speaks about daily corporate study of Torah: "These are the things, the fruits of which a man enjoys in this world, while the stock remains for him for the world to come" (*Authorised Daily Prayer Book* 5).

Maimonides believed that we express our love for God by dedicating ourselves to the study of Torah. Constant study is like the constant preoccupation of a lover with the beloved (*Hilkhot Teshuvah* 10:3). The converse is also true; constant study itself leads to and fosters the love for God. The prophet Hoshea (Hosea) understood this. He saw the people dying from lack of knowledge of God. The effect of this lack was that their love was "like a morning cloud, like dew that disappears quickly" (Hos. 6:4–6). Their desperate need was to know him.

The traditional way is to gather in pairs in order to study. The belief is that "A man should acquire a friend for himself to read Scripture with him, to study Mishnah with him, eat with him, drink with him, and disclose his secrets to him" (Cohen, 198, quoting *Sifre Deuteronomy*). Leo Rosten recalls the old days of European Jewry: "Virtually *all* of male Jewry used to participate in a perpetual seminar—on the Torah and the Talmud" (Rosten, 69). The need for this kind of conversation was so great that when workers found leisure time to get together in intimate groups they would urge one another to "tell me a little Torah" (Rosten, 70).

Walking, Lying Down, and Rising Up

Hillel taught that one should recite the Sh'ma at those times when people normally go to bed in the evening and get up in the morning. Shammai, his contemporary and rival, interpreted the direction more literally. He taught that one should recite the Sh'ma in the evening while lying down, and in the morning while standing. Certainly the understanding, from early times, has been that there should be a twice-daily recitation. One way of looking at this is to say that in the morning one is taking upon oneself the yoke of Torah. In the evening we remember to whom we belong, and we dedicate our rest to him. It is likely that the institution of morning and evening prayer had its origins in this instruction.

The direction also has a wider implication. God expects us to discuss our duty to him (to love him with heart, soul, and might) as we walk in the way, as well as when we lie down to rest at night and rise in the morning (Lipson, *The Hebrew Christian*, Summer 1975. 52).

It seems that there is no time, and no place, that is inappropriate for talking about God and his Word. It is always seemly to share our love of God with one another.

Yeshua

There is no time when Torah should not be a part of our lives. We have already seen that this is a tenet of Judaism, and it certainly was a principle of Yeshua's earthly life. We find him, even as a lad, saying to his parents, "Didn't you know that I had to be concerning myself with my Father's affairs?" (Luke 2:49). Yeshua the rabbi concerned himself with his Father's affairs at all times, in all places, in all situations. He taught his disciples "on the hoof." He spoke of God's Way when a guest at table. He expounded God's Word using everyday incidents and sights as a starting point. It might be a field of flowers, a whitewashed tomb, an emotional woman, a family tragedy, a squabble among the *talmidim*, or a ceremony in the Temple. Anything might develop into talking about God and his Torah when sitting at home, when traveling on the road.

The conversation on the Emmaus road is a prime example. After his Resurrection Yeshua did not have to travel anywhere. He could appear wherever he chose. He made a decision to walk that road on that day. His intention was to explain "to them the things that can be found throughout the *Tanakh* concerning himself" (Luke 24:27). He did this in true rabbinical fashion, while "traveling on the road". He revealed himself while sharing in a meal.

This concept of "anywhere, any time" is utterly foreign to western culture. There is a belief that one must keep the sacred and the secular in separate compartments. Religion should not interfere with business, and socializing should not detract from holiness. I remember as a girl, in England, being taught that in polite society one should never discuss religion and politics at the meal table. Judaism sees things quite differently, and Yeshua was a Jew. In this matter he was in tune with common Jewish practice.

The First *Talmidim*

The first generation of Messianic teachers developed the theme that speech is inseparable from a way of life. Yeshua himself had said that what comes out of a person reveals what is within. The early translators of the Bible into English used the word "conversation" to indicate "way of life." It has naturally evolved to indicate speech.

Sha'ul directed his flock to watch their speech. It should be gracious and interesting (Col. 4:6), and it should be wholesome (Titus 2:8). Timothy, as a young leader, was to set his people a good example in speech and in his whole manner of living (1 Tim. 4:12). Words and life must match up, or there is no integrity.

Kefa did not deal with the tongue as a separate issue. His concern was that believers in Yeshua should live totally holy lives. For him, the ancient call of God was still pre-eminent. God had said, "Be holy, for I am holy" (Lev. 11:44). Therefore, he said, "Following the Holy One who called you, become holy yourselves in your entire way of life" (1 Pet. 1:15). True godliness will transform the whole life; no area will be left untouched. This quality of life, he believed, would speak volumes to those who did not believe in the God of Isra'el. Associates and family members alike would be affected, and might even come to believe in God's Word (1 Pet. 2:12; 3:1–2).

Ya'akov (James), too, taught the importance of a "good way of life" to back up knowledge and understanding (James 3:13). He was under no illusions, though, about the importance of speech. His diatribe against evil speaking in chapter three was perhaps stimulated by a specific situation, but it remains apposite. The tongue that blesses God may not also speak evil against people, who are made in God's image. One cannot switch holiness on and off at will.

Yochanan, with penetrating insight, saw through to the heart of the matter. After all, the direction concerning talking is a development of the command to love God. That is the greatest commandment. Yes, we can—and should—love God with our speech. Speech, however, cannot be considered in isolation from the whole life. Yochanan, therefore, cut to the chase. "Children, let us not love with words and talk, but with actions and in reality!" (1 John 3:18). When we love, it must be with the things we do as well as the words we say.

For Thought

Talking is more than mere recitation. It is a means of communication with one another and with God. This is how understanding deepens and faith grows. Through conversation and social intercourse relationships develop, both with one another and with God.

Is this direction about personal evangelism? I do not think so—at least, not directly. It is not about "speaking a word for the Lord" and feeling guilt-tripped if we do not. It is about living an integrated life in which God and his Word and ways will naturally salt our language and conversation. The important word here is "naturally." This very naturalness affects those with whom we mix and creates a challenge for them. That is my experience.

The life we live speaks as loudly as the words we say. If life and words do not match up, the effect will be negative. Particularly is this so in our homes. The rabbis were wise to make a point of this. Visitors may be quick to pick up the atmosphere we create. The "vibes" will have a deeper impact than the words!

Language is so important to us. When we love, we long to hear the words "I love you" from the beloved. They must be spoken. Without those words there is no security in the relationship. Of course Yeshua knew that Kefa loved him, but he wanted to hear it said—and he knew that Kefa needed to say it (John 21:15). Words are not, however, enough in isolation. They must be accompanied by practical demonstrations of love. These demonstrations need to be reciprocal.

It is like this with the believer's relationship to God. He loves us. He has told us so. He has demonstrated his love in delivering his people Isra'el from Egypt and in giving his Son, Isra'el's Messiah, for us all. He shows his love in countless other ways to each one individually. How, therefore, are we to respond? We may *feel* we love him, we may *say* we love him. We want our lives to *show* that we love him. As we walk with him, study his Word, and share our findings with one another we shall get to know him better, and discover what pleases him. That is how love relationships develop.

A Prayer

Lord, I bless and thank you for the gift of your Word. Help me with each passing day to know and understand it better. Then I shall know and understand you better. I need your Holy Spirit power to live it more truly, your Holy Spirit grace to reflect its beauty and holiness, and your Holy Spirit freedom to talk about it at all times.

Eternal God, open my lips, that my mouth may declare Your praise. (*Siddur Lev Chadash,* 52).

> It is good to give thanks to ADONAI
> and sing praises to your name, 'Elyon,
> to tell in the morning about your grace
> and at night about your faithfulness. (Ps. 92:2-3 (1–2))

Eternal God, may the words of Torah taste sweet to us and to all Isra'el, that we and our children, and all the children of Your people, may come to know You by studying Torah (*Siddur lev Chadash,* 131).

Blessed are you, O Lord our God, King of the universe, who has given us the gift of language. Grant that we may use that gift wisely, graciously, and lovingly.

CHAPTER 15

Tie Them As A Sign

קְשַׁרְתָּם לְאוֹת

K'shar'tem l'ot

"Tie them on your hand as a sign, put them at the front of a headband round your forehead" (Deut. 6:8).

"The object of this commandment is to direct our thoughts to God and his goodness" (Friedlander, 331).

The *Tefillin*

Jewish people through the generations have interpreted this direction in a literal way. They were to bind God's words on the hand, and place them on the forehead by means of a headband. The Talmud indeed teaches that God gave the instructions concerning tefillin to Moshe on Sinai as part of the Oral Law (*Men.* 35a).

The tefillin are square boxes, with straps, made of leather from kosher animals, usually cattle or sheep; as the Talmud says: "How do we know that tefillin may be written only on the skins of a clean [edible] animal? Because it is written, that the Law of the Lord may be in thy mouth" (*Shab.* 108a). They are usually black, and the boxes are usually one to four centimeters wide. One is worn on the forehead and one on the left upper arm. The letter *shin* is embossed on the head tefillin, representing the word *Shaddai*—Almighty. If they have leather covers for protection when not in use, one will be inscribed שֶׁל יָד (*shel yad*—for the hand), and the other שֶׁל רֹאשׁ (*shel rosh*—for the head).

Inside each box are four tiny parchment scrolls, each containing a Torah passage: Exodus 13:1–10 concerns the keeping of *Pesach*; Exodus 13:11–16 concerns the redemption of the first-born, and concludes with the words, "This will serve as a sign on your hand and at the front of a headband around your forehead that with a strong hand ADONAI brought us out of Egypt"; Deuteronomy 6:4–9 is the first part of the Sh'ma, which includes the words, "Tie them [these words] on your hand as a sign, put them at the front of a headband around your forehead"; Deuteronomy 6:13–21 contains the command for Isra'el to be faithful to ADONAI, their God, throughout their generations. There is also the promise of blessing in the Land, conditional on their faithfulness.

These passages, therefore, contain many of the basic tenets of Judaism, tenets which are at the heart of the opening section of the Sh'ma: faith in the One God; the command to love God with the whole of one's being; the deliverance of Isra'el from Egypt; Isra'el's inheritance of the promised Land. Also contained in there is the concept of reward and punishment, together with directions concerning various practices that distinguish Isra'el from other peoples.

The Wearing of Tefillin

A Jewish man will don the tefillin for his morning prayers. It is possible that in early times they were worn all day. Josephus, writing in the second century C.E., mentions the practice (*Antiquities* 4, 8:13). However, very few were doing this by mishnaic and talmudic times. The practice may have declined in order not to profane the tefillin by wearing them in defiled places. It may also have been in order to avoid religious persecution. The change of custom was perhaps a consequence of the dispersion of the Jewish people after the Roman destruction of Jerusalem.

Incidentally, the rabbis have discouraged, even forbidden, women to lay tefillin. This may not always have been so. Indeed, there is reference in the Talmud to women laying tefillin (*Eir.* 96a).

It is customary to wear tefillin during the recital of the *Amidah* and the Sh'ma. Indeed, one rabbi taught that "If one recites the Sh'ma without tefillin it is as if he bore false witness against himself" (*Ber.* 14b). However, they are not worn on Sabbaths and festivals, perhaps because they might detract from the sanctity of the day. These days are themselves signs, so it is unnecessary to don the signs of tefillin (*Men.* 36b). Because they are an adornment of glory, it is not appropriate to wear them on days of mourning.

The Laying (putting on) of *Tefillin*

The manner of laying tefillin is specifically ordered in every detail. The whole object of the exercise is to direct one's thoughts to God, his holiness and his goodness - that clearing of the mind so important to Maimonides. It is necessary, therefore, to be careful and reverent. The two boxes are of equal importance, representing as they do the head and the heart. To emphasize this, the hand tefillin is part donned, then the head tefillin, then the hand is completed.

While winding the hand strap round the middle finger of the left hand one recites words from the prophet Hoshea:

> I will betroth you to me forever;
> yes, I will betroth you to me
> in righteousness, in justice,
> in grace and in compassion;
> I will betroth you to me in faithfulness,
> and you will know ADONAI. (Hos. 2:19–20 (21–22))

The strap is wound round the finger three times, to correspond to the three times the word "betroth" occurs in this passage. This forms a ring round the finger, so reiterating and renewing the love relationship between God and Isra'el.

The strap is then so tied round the left hand as to form the letter שׁ (*shin*). This represents *Shaddai*—one of God's sacred names. That brings God's holiness to mind, and leads to the tefillin themselves being regarded as sacred. One does not sleep or eat while wearing them, neither does one enter the bathroom. When they wear out one must dispose of them in a respectful way.

The laying of head tefillin is completed by tying the strap at the back of the head with a knot resembling the letter ד—the first letter of *rosh* (head). The hand tefillin strap has a loop resembling the letter י—the first letter of *yad* (hand).

There is a *b'rakhah* one makes while laying tefillin: "Blessed are you, O Lord our God, King of the universe, who has sanctified us by your commandments, and commanded us to lay tefillin." Then, at some point during his prayers, the worshipper will recite the two passages from Exodus.

The Symbolism of Tefillin

The word *tefillah* means, literally, prayer. The root of the word can mean "to judge, to examine oneself." It could also mean "sign," or "testimony." However, Steinsaltz declares that the direction to wear tefillin does not necessarily have anything to do with prayer; it stands alone, in its own right (Steinsaltz, *A Guide to Jewish Prayer* 349). Perhaps the connection between the laying of tefillin and prayer is simply a tradition that has developed since the days when they were worn all the time.

The tefillin of the head is called *Totafot* (a reminder). It is as if the head is crowned—a reminder of our connection to God who is the royal Sovereign. One is in submission to divine authority. One's thoughts should be concentrated on God and what pleases him. The head that has worn *Totafot* ought not to harbor thoughts or ambitions which are impure. The tefillin are a reminder of our commitment to God and our duty to live a life of service.

The tefillin of the arm is called *Ot* (a sign). The hand that has been sanctified by the laying of the *Ot* may not be employed in degenerate actions, to harm others or displease God. The heart, near which the *Ot* lies, is to generate desires and emotions, which spring from an all-consuming love of God. The tefillin are a reflection of that love, and a reminder to nourish it always.

The two tefillin together, therefore, signify that the hand, head, and heart are all to be devoted to God who made us. We are to love him with all that we are–with all our heart, all our being, and all our resources. They also symbolize bonds. We are bound to God our Redeemer because of what happened at the Exodus. We are bound to God the Holy One, because of what happened on Sinai. As Steinsaltz puts it: "This glorious combination of crown and chains thus ties together our complete, total relationship as both sons and servants to our Father and King" (Steinsaltz, *A Guide to Jewish Prayer* 358).

The laying of tefillin is a personal act rather than a communal one. However, everything in Jewish life has communal significance. The Talmud tells us that the tefillin, laid by individual members of Isra'el, are a source of strength to the whole nation (*Ber.* 6a).

Yeshua

Did Yeshua lay tefillin? Perhaps the question one should ask is, "Why should he not?" In his day men wore them all the time. They were an accepted part of Jewish life. Surely if he had not conformed in this matter, some of his accusers would have brought it up against him.

The truth is, however, we do not know. Tefillin are only mentioned once in connection with Yeshua, and that is in Matthew 23:5. Incidentally, the word in most English translations is "phylacteries." That is an unfortunate rendering, because it comes from a Greek word meaning "a charm." The implication is that the wearing of tefillin is a superstitious practice. It is not; it is a biblical practice.

Yeshua is not condemning the use of tefillin. He is talking about those who make a performance of the ritual, whose main concern is that they look good to other people. They do things in such a way as to appear more religious, more holy, than others. He does not condemn the wearing of tefillin. He condemns their misuse. They were to be a reminder that one is in the presence of the only God, that one's thoughts should be directed to him. They were to be a sign that one loved this unique, holy, yet personal God with all one's faculties—mental, emotional, and physical. What a travesty to turn the practice into a piece of exhibitionism!

For Thought

The practices concerning tefillin may seem strange, archaic, and utterly foreign, to many readers. Some Messianic Jews may feel uncomfortable, embarrassed, about this chapter. Others will feel that they should take on these customs. They are, after all, biblical in origin, though not in much of the detail. You may be influenced by a desire to identify with your people. Messianic tradition does not help us. We simply do not know how long this practice survived among the early believers.

Whether one conforms to the practice or not, Yeshua urges us to look behind the practice to the motive. Why do I do this? Why do I not do that? Who is my judge—God, or human beings? How do I stand with regard to what Yeshua called "the first and greatest commandment"? Do I love him with all my heart, mind, and strength?

In Secret

Yeshua's teaching here is in keeping with his words about fasting, about giving. The Church has rediscovered fasting during the past few decades. Is there a tendency, however subtle, for fasting to be considered a mark of holiness among believers? What would Yeshua say about that? In some communities, people's giving is public. What would Yeshua say about that? I think we know the answer to those questions.

> Be careful not to parade your acts of tzedakah [righteousness] in front of people in order to be seen by them! If you do, you have no reward from your Father in heaven. So, when you do tzedakah, don't announce it with trumpets to win people's praise, like the hypocrites in the synagogues and on the streets. Yes! I tell you, they have their reward already! But you, when you do tzedakah, don't even let your left hand know what your right hand is doing. Then your tzedakah will be in secret; and your Father, who sees what you do in secret, will reward you. (Matt. 6:1–4)

> When you pray, go into your room, close the door, and pray to your Father in secret. (Matt. 6:6)

> When you fast, don't go around looking miserable, like the hypocrites. They make sour faces so that people will know they are fasting…when you fast, wash your face and groom yourself, so that no one will know you are fasting—except your Father, who is with you in secret. (Matt. 6:16–18)

Some things are private, between the worshipper and God himself. They are not for display before others, to create an impression of super-spirituality. Followers of Yeshua are not to be like those who practice this kind of exhibitionism.

Yeshua said that there was a special blessing for the "pure in heart." They would see God (Matt. 5:8). I wonder if perhaps he had Psalm 51 in mind as he said those words. David knew that there was no hope for him unless his sin with *Bat-sheva* (Bathsheba) was confessed, repented, and forgiven. So he pleaded for cleansing. The only way his joy in the Lord could be renewed was for God to give him a pure heart. That means an open, transparent heart, free from hypocrisy. Our God, who is holy and true, will have us open, transparent, free from pretense in all our dealings, both with himself and with the people around us.

Another of David's psalms speaks of this sincerity and openness:

> Who may go up to the mountain of ADONAI?
> Who can stand in his holy place?
> Those with clean hands and pure hearts,
> who don't make vanities the purpose of their lives
> or swear oaths just to deceive. (Psalm 24:3–4)

Discipline and Devotion

Many of us lack discipline in the matter of our prayer life. The practice of donning the tefillin, carefully, in the prescribed manner, might be a tremendous help here. You will know that now it is time to shut out all other thoughts. Your family will know not to intrude, because you have withdrawn to spend time with God.

Since the Reformation, Protestant believers have looked askance at the use of signs and symbols as aids to prayer. Have we, perhaps, thrown out the baby with the bath water? If you have a difficulty with settling down to prayer, why not try finding some visible sign to yourself that separates this time away from what went before and what comes after? It need not necessarily be something alien to your culture and personality.

A Prayer

Lord, I want my life to be totally free of hypocrisy. Forgive me that I so often hide my sin, dryness, and pain behind a mask. I want people to think well of me—especially my fellow believers. Sometimes I even put on an act in public worship! Please skim away the impurities in my heart and make it pure. Please burn out the sin in my life and make it clean.

> My sin confronts me all the time....
> Turn away your face from my sins,
> and blot out all my crimes.
>
> Create in me a clean heart, God;
> renew in me a resolute spirit....
> Restore my joy in your salvation...
>
> Then my tongue will sing
> about your righteousness—
> ADONAI, open my lips;
> then my mouth will praise you. (Psalm 51:3(5); 9–10
> (10–11); 14–15(1516))

Blessed are you, O Lord our God, King of the universe, who delights in your people's repentance, who forgives, restores, and renews.

CHAPTER 16

Write Them

K'tav'tam

"Write them on the door-frames of your house and on your gates" (Deut. 6:9).

The Talmud tells the story of a proselyte (convert to Judaism) who explained the mezuzah:

> According to universal custom, the mortal king dwells within, and his servants keep guard on him without; but [in the case of] the Holy One, blessed be He, it is His servants who dwell within whilst He keeps guard on them from without; as it is said: 'The Lord shall guard thy going out and thy coming in from this time forth and for evermore.'[Ps. 121:8] (Av. Zar. 11a)

The Mezuzah

The word actually means "door-post," but it has come to signify a small case fixed to the doorpost on the right-hand side as you enter the house. It is fixed at about head height, in a slanting position, the upper part inclining toward the inside of the house or room. This case contains a tiny parchment scroll on which are written Deuteronomy 6:4–9 and 11:13–20. Those are the first two paragraphs of the Sh'ma. One can see the word שַׁדַּי (Shaddai) on the outside of the mezuzah. Many homes have mezuzot on the doorposts of the living rooms and bedrooms as well. The appearance and design are infinitely variable, from subtle and antique to modern and perhaps garish!

They were to fix mezuzot to doors and gates. That means homes and cities, for in ancient times the cities had gates. There have been disputes about which places should have a mezuzah, and the Talmud discusses the question (*Yoma* 10, 11). Should the bathroom have one? What about the *sukkah* (the temporary shelter built for the Festival of *Sukkot*)? Should there be one on the cattle-shed? Most rabbis have agreed that a place that has a recognized religious purpose is sanctified by its very nature and usage, and so does not need a mezuzah.

When first fixing the mezuzah, one prays, "Blessed are you, O Lord our God, King of the universe, who has sanctified us by your commandments and commanded us to affix the mezuzah." Then the practice is to touch it and kiss the fingers on entering and leaving the house. At the same time one prays, "May God keep my going out and my coming in from now on and forever."

According to the Talmud, women are not exempt from this *mitzvah* (*Ber.* 20b); it is incumbent on everyone. "He who is observant of mezuzah will merit a beautiful dwelling," said Rabbi Huna (*Shab.* 23b). By contrast, he who does not observe this commandment is considered an "*am ha-aretz* [earthly, unspiritual man]" (*Ber.* 47b). Such a person is in one of the seven groups of people who are "banned by heaven" (*Pes.* 113b).

Symbolism

The presence of the mezuzah is a sign that a house is consecrated to God—as indeed it must be, if we are loving God with all our resources. The word *Shaddai*, which we can see on the outside of the mezuzah, is a reminder that Almighty God watches over the house and all who enter it. Touching the mezuzah as we enter is an acknowledgment that we are treading, so to speak, on holy ground. Doing so as we leave reminds us to commit the house to the protection of the Almighty.

The mezuzah, then, is a sign of God's presence, and particularly of his watchful care for us. Here is another rabbinic legend:

> Artaban sent to Rabbenu a priceless pearl, and said to him, 'Send me a precious object of equal value.' R. Judah sent him a mezuzah. He said to him, 'I sent you a priceless gift, and you send me something worth a penny.' R. Judah replied, 'Our re-

spective gifts cannot be compared. Moreover, you sent me something which I must guard, but I sent you something which, when you sleep, will guard you, as it is said, "When thou walkest, it will lead thee, when thou liest down, it will watch over thee, and when thou awakest, it will talk with thee." (Montefiore, 133).

We can see, from this story, how easy it has been for the mezuzah to be regarded as a sort of charm. Sometimes people have thought that it guarantees God's protection just by its presence, regardless of any obedience to the injunctions it contains. Maimonides considered it necessary to speak against superstitious practices around the mezuzah. In the twentieth century, Cohen also commented that in the popular mind the mezuzah had became an amulet, which conveyed divine protection (Cohen, 160–61).

The mezuzah is also a sign of our responsibilities to God. This command is a part of the Sh'ma. It serves to remind us of the unity and uniqueness of God, and of our duty to love him with all that we are and have. Maimonides expressed it like this: "By the commandment of the mezuzah man is reminded, when coming or going, of the unity of God, and is aroused to the love of Him" (Mishneh Torah, Tefillin 6:13). The God who is present is also holy, and his holiness must affect all who enter the house, all that is done within it. When things go well for the family we must not be arrogant; when things go badly we must not turn aside from God by falling into despair or rebellion.

The wearing of tefillin is an individual responsibility. The practice of observing the mezuzah is communal. The whole household is covered by this, involved in it. Remembering that gates are the boundary of the city, not the home, we realize too that the meaning is even wider. God's ideal is that the whole community should acknowledge and love him.

The Two Passages

There is significance in the two passages appointed to comprise the mezuzah. The first is known as שְׁמַע (Sh'ma—hear). The second is וְהָיָה אִם שָׁמֹעַ (ADONAI im Sh'ma—if you listen carefully to the

LORD). The first passage speaks of who God is and what he requires of us; the second presents us with the choice we face, as God's people. If we listen and obey, we shall be blessed in the Land he gives us to inhabit. The alternative is that we do not; we let ourselves be seduced into turning aside and worshipping other gods. In that event God tells us that his anger will burn against us, and we will "pass away from the good land" he gave our people. We remember that Moshe told the people at the end of his life: "This is not a trivial matter for you; on the contrary, it is your life! Through it you will live long in the land you are crossing the *Yarden* [Jordan] to possess" (Deut. 32:47).

The rabbis have seen here the principle of reward and punishment. God will never reject his people, but he will withdraw his blessing from the generation that turns aside. "Therefore," says the Lord, "You are to store up these words of mine in your heart and in all your being" (Deut. 11:18). That is why it is important to speak of them constantly, to teach them to the next generation. The purpose of laying tefillin and placing the mezuzah is that they may be aids and stimuli to this laying up of God's words in our hearts and our being. The purpose of laying up his words is that we might respond to him in love always, never deviating from his paths, never turning from his face.

The house or city with a mezuzah on its entrance ought to be a place where, above all else, God is central. He is the source of all prosperity. He is the goal of all endeavor. He is the center of all affection. The command to love God with all we are and have is for the community as well as the individual.

Yeshua

There is no mention of the mezuzah in the *B'rit Hadashah*. It is likely, though, that the Messiah was familiar with the practice. Josephus, who lived in the years immediately after the death of Yeshua, seems to speak of it as a well-established custom (*Antiquities,* 4:8:13). Yeshua was hardly in a position to fix a mezuzah on the doorpost of his own home; during his years of ministry he had no home. "The foxes have holes, and the birds flying about have nests, but the Son of Man has no home of his own" (Matt. 8:20).

Receiving hospitality

There is, however, an echo of this *mitzvah* in some other words re-corded by Matthew. He was sending out the twelve to an itinerant ministry. How would they deal with the matter of hospitality?

> When you come to a town or village, look for someone trust-worthy and stay with him until you leave. When you enter someone's household, say, '*Shalom aleychem* [Peace be with you]!' If the home deserves it, let your *shalom* rest on it; if not, let your *shalom* return to you. (Matt. 10:11–13)

There is an echo here of David's message to Naval: "Long life and *shalom* to you, *shalom* to your household, and *shalom* to ev-erything that is yours!" (1 Sam. 25:6). This was a customary form of greeting from very early times.

The principle is similar. As they entered a godly home, the *talmidim* were to pray that the blessing of God's *shalom* would rest upon it. It was not for them to follow up that blessing; God him-self would know if they had made a mistake. It was for him alone to withdraw the blessing; it is his prerogative to give or withdraw *shalom*.

If You Listen Carefully

There is a promise and a warning contained in the second para-graph of the Sh'ma, which is part of the mezuzah scroll. If God's people listen carefully to his words and obey them, he will prosper their ways. If they turn aside and do not listen carefully and obey, God will withdraw his blessing from them.

Yeshua told a story—a parable—about this:

> Everyone who hears these words of mine and acts on them will be like a sensible man who built his house on bedrock. The rain fell, the rivers flooded, the winds blew and beat against that house, but it didn't collapse, because its foundation was on rock. But everyone who hears these words of mine and does not act on them will be like a stupid man who built his house on sand. The rain fell, the rivers flooded, the wind blew and

beat against that house, and it collapsed—and its collapse was
horrendous! (Matt. 7:24–27)

Why did the man's house fall? It fell because he heard the
words of Yeshua but did not act on them. This is precisely the
warning given in Deuteronomy chapter 11, but with one significant difference. Yeshua was speaking about listening to and obey-
ing his own words. In echoing the thought of the Sh'ma, Yeshua
was surely making one of his oblique claims about his own identity. Listening to his words is equivalent to listening to God's
words. To ignore his words is to ignore God's words. To turn
away from Yeshua is to turn away from God himself.

Is it any wonder that the crowds were amazed at the way Yeshua
taught? Matthew comments, "He was not instructing them like their
Torah-teachers but as one who had authority himself" (Matt. 7:29).
The listening crowd saw the significance of what Yeshua was saying.
Who indeed was this man who claimed, and exuded, an authority
way beyond that of the rabbis and religious leaders?

These questions about the identity of Yeshua still remain today.
At the heart of the Jewish-Christian debate lies the one issue that really matters: Who is Yeshua? Yes, he was an observant Jewish man.
Yes, he was a rabbi of extraordinary charisma. Was he, however,
more than that? Was he the Messiah? Was he—and this is the fundamental question—the divine Son of God. Was he—is he—part of
that Godhead about which the Sh'ma says "The Lord is One"?

For Thought

There are three thoughts that we might consider, arising out of this
study of the mezuzah. First, let us look at the concepts of home
and community. The mezuzah marks out the household and the
community that belongs to God. It is, however, primarily a sign
for those who belong, not for those who do not. It is generally acknowledged that Jewish people have always been better at community than the Gentiles among whom they have lived. I believe
Messianic congregations are better at community than many gentile
Christian churches, although there are many that demonstrate the
same sort of community found among the Jewish people. The

present-day stress on evangelism has biblical authority; if, however, it is not supported by strong, cohesive, mutually loving, and supportive communities of believers, the evangelism lacks credibility. Jewish people who become believers in Yeshua have missed the warmth of this element of community in gentile churches. If we do not feel loved and safe in our congregation, how can we feel motivated to bring someone else along?

Second, there is the issue of promise and warning, of reward and punishment. Yeshua echoes the Sh'ma in saying that blessing is not automatic. Faith—trusting belief—leads to everlasting life. Yeshua, however, pointed out to his disciples that true blessing from God is for the poor in spirit, the mourners, the meek, the merciful, the pure in heart, the peacemakers, those who endure suffering in the pursuit of righteousness (Matt. 5:1–10). He has words for communities of believers too. The first chapters of Revelation show his high expectation of their faith and conduct, his withdrawal of blessing if they grow cold in their love, turn away from his words. Believers in Yeshua do not earn their salvation; they do, however, have to work it out, as Sha'ul said, "with fear and trembling" (Phil. 2:12).

Third, we need to consider the identity of Yeshua. Many books have been written about this. I suppose that for most Messianic Jews and gentile Christians the issue comes down to the Resurrection. If the Resurrection was a historical fact, Yeshua's claims are verified. If it was not then, as Sha'ul said, "Your trust is useless, and you are still in your sins" (1 Cor. 15:17).

Yeshua's identity is, however, more than a theological matter. Who is he to you, to me? Many believers know him first as Savior. Have we ever explored what that might mean beyond the initial experience of saving faith? What does he save me from today?

Yeshua's identification with the God of the Sh'ma opens up awesome vistas of who he is and what he can be to us. Look at the titles of God found in the Hebrew Scriptures. Study and consider them. Realize that for each of those titles, Yeshua might say, "That's me!"

If Yeshua is co-equal with the Father, we must give his words equal weight. The converse is also true; if Yeshua is part of God, then he is eternal, and therefore has always been speaking to us in God's words. The Hebrew Scriptures are as much his word as the *B'rit Hadashah*.

Yeshua made some awesome promises to his followers. If he is who he claimed to be, those promises are valid. How seriously do we take them? He makes extraordinary demands on his followers. If he is who he claimed to be, those demands are justified. How seriously do we take them?

A Prayer

I treasure your word in my heart,
so that I won't sin against you ...
Make me understand the ways of your precepts...
Bend my heart toward your instructions. (Ps. 119:11; 27; 36)

So often, Lord, my reading of your words seems like a chore. Please restore to me the delight they once gave me. Show me, each day, how to live my life as your words are directing me. I want to submit to the authority and power of your words. I want your words to keep on changing me.

Blessed are you, O Lord our God, King of the universe, whose Word is a two-edged sword. May that sword pierce the hardness of my heart, and direct my steps in your ways.

CHAPTER 17

Look, Remember And Obey

רְאִיתֶם וּזְכַרְתֶּם וַעֲשִׂיתֶם

R'item v'z'kar'tem v'asitem

"Speak to the people of Isra'el, instructing them to make, through all their generations, tzitziyot on the corners of their garments" (Num. 15:38).

"Beloved is Israel [to God], for the Holy One, blessed be He, surrounded them with commandments of tefillin for their heads, tefillin for their arms, tzitzit for their clothing, and mezuzot for their doors" (*Men.* 43b).

God's commands are given, not to bind his people in chains, but as a mark of his special love. They are given us in order to strengthen our love of God, to help us know and express our praise and delight in him. The Psalmist said, "I praise you seven times a day" (Ps. 119:164). Those seven times, says the Talmud, refer to the seven precepts: the four fringes, the two tefillin, and the mezuzah (*Men.* 43b).

The Third Paragraph

The third section of the Sh'ma, found in Numbers chapter 15, deals with tzitziyot. The people of Isra'el were to put tzitziyot on the corners of their garments through all their generations. They were to look at them in order to remember and obey all God's commandments, and to be holy unto their God. This commandment is not meant to be a burden; it is given to God's people in order to help them.

"Look at them," says God. Our heavenly Teacher is a great believer in visual aids! Hirsch points out that the root meaning of the word *tzitzit* is actually "to appear in visual form" (Hirsch, 181).

The Garment

In ancient times, this commandment applied to the normal everyday outer garment worn by Jewish men. It was not a special garment; it was made special by the tzitziyot. It was normal to wear a four-cornered garment. In course of time, dress styles changed, and the four-cornered garment went out of fashion. The practice of attaching the fringes could have lapsed at that point. The problem was solved by developing the custom of retaining the garment, with its fringes, for prayer use. From that time, Jewish people have regarded the *tallit* (prayer shawl) as a sacred, rather than an everyday garment.

The *tallit* is a rectangular garment of no fixed size, though it should be large enough to wrap oneself in (Steinsaltz, *Talmud reference Guide* 249). There is a fringe along each end, and a tassel on each corner. It must not be made of a mixture of wool and linen, in obedience to the words in Torah: "You are not to wear clothing woven with two kinds of thread, wool and linen together" (Deut. 22:11). Traditionally the color has been sober—white, with bands near the ends of black or blue, but today many *tallitot* are more brightly colored. The fringes should be of the same color as the garment, to avoid any suggestion of frivolity. However, it is not wrong to wear a *tallit* with a beautiful fringe. Doing so is one of the ways one can glorify God and give him pleasure by one's own enjoyment of the *mitzvah*. The blue thread specified in Numbers 15 is not present today because the recipe for the correct blue dye has been lost, although some claim to know it. The tassels are of no fixed length, but there is a prescribed minimum length (*Men.* 42a). The composition of the tassels is most specifically ordered.

The *Tallit Katan*

During the middle ages, in times of persecution, Jewish men began to wear a much smaller *tallit*, which slipped over the head, as an undergarment. Many still wear this *tallit katan* (small prayer shawl) all the time, with just the tzitziyot showing. Even very small boys, who might be too young to wear the *tallit*, will wear a *tallit katan* as a normal item of clothing.

The *Tzitziyot*

The *tzitzit* comprises four threads, three of equal length, one longer. These are looped through a hole near the corner of the *tallit*, forming a tassel of eight threads. They are knotted just below the edge of the *tallit*. The longer thread—the *shammash* (servant)— is then wound round the others a specific number of times, then another knot is tied. This process is repeated until there are five knots. The remaining strands are left hanging loosely. It was the *shammash* that was originally blue.

Letters in Hebrew have a numerical value, and great significance is often given to these values. The eight threads plus the five knots plus the numerical value of the word *tzitzit* add up to 613— the number of laws in the Torah.

The number of windings of the *shammash* is also significant. In most communities it is seven plus eight plus eleven plus thirteen, making a total of thirty-nine. That is the numerical value of the words *Ha-Shem Echad* (the Lord is One). In some communities the windings are ten then five then six then five, making a total of twenty-six. That is the numerical value of the Tetragrammaton—יהוה (YHVH).

Rashi believed the eight threads represented the eight days between the people of Isra'el leaving Egypt and their song of praise on the far side of the Sea of Reeds. The blue thread, he said, represented the sorrow of the Egyptians' bereavement of their firstborn (Rashi, *Numbers* 77a).

Hertz saw the blue as a reminder of the sky, leading to thoughts of God's throne in heaven (Hertz, *Numbers* 159).

The Four Corners

Rashi saw the four corners as representing the four different terms God used to describe the deliverance from Egypt in Exodus chapter 6. These terms were: "I will bring you forth...I will deliver you...I will redeem you...I will take you out." (Rashi, *Numbers* 77a). These promises are the basis for the custom of drinking four cups of wine at the Passover *seder*.

Others have seen in them the four corners of the earth, the entire universe. Hirsch said they remind us that when we look in any direction we can remember God and his Law (Hirsch, 182).

Who Wears the *Tallit*?

This has been the subject of much discussion. One rabbi was of the opinion that women as well as men should wear the fringes (*Sukk*.11a). This view is by no means unanimous. Another rabbi declared women exempt, because the precept is dependent on a fixed time. Women are customarily excused from all such precepts because of the calls of domestic duties. Others again, however, have thought differently: "Our Rabbis taught: All must observe the law of tzitzit; priests, Levites, and Israelites, proselytes, women and slaves" (*Men.* 43a).

Today, it is not usual for women to wear *tallitot*, though they may in some less orthodox communities. Other customs vary, too. Some say that boys should wear them once they old enough to know how to use them (*Arachin* 2b). Some say only married men should wear them, while others limit the occasions on which single men may wear them.

When is the *Tallit* Worn?

Customs vary from community to community. Generally, however, one wears it during morning services, throughout the *Yom Kippur* services, and on certain ceremonial occasions. Those called up for the Reading of Torah will wear a *tallit*, as will one pronouncing the priestly blessing, and one who officiates at a circumcision.

The important direction regarding the tzitziyot is that one is to look at them. That means they must be visible. One does not, therefore, wear the *tallit* in the hours of darkness. The traditional ruling was that there must be enough light to be able to discern the blue thread.

The *tallit* is regarded as a sacred garment and, as such, is not to be worn in unsuitable places—for instance, in the bathroom.

How is the *Tallit* Worn?

As he puts on the *tallit*, the worshipper recites words from Psalm 36:

> How precious, God, is your grace!
> People take refuge in the shadow of your wings,...

For with you is the fountain of life;
in your light we see light. (Ps. 36: 7(8); 9(10))

Before the reading of the Sh'ma, the worshipper will gather the four tzitziyot together. This may symbolize the ingathering of the exiles and the bringing of blessing and peace. During the recital of the Sh'ma, he will look at the tzitziyot, and kiss them.

During prayers in the synagogue, sometimes worshippers will cover their heads with the *tallit*, in order to make a private place of prayer, and concentrate without distraction.

The Purpose of the *Tzitziyot*

"It is to be a *tzitzit* for you to look at" (Numbers 15:39). The fringes are primarily for us to look at, in order that we might remember and obey all the other commandments. They have therefore become a general reminder of all God's commandments. As such, the rabbis have seen them as a sort of security against sinning—an antidote to the urges of our baser nature. We look at them and we strengthen our resolve to be the holy people of our calling. This is part of the outworking of our love for God, which must affect the way we live as well as the words we say and the emotions we feel. We want to love him with all that we are. That is why a past rabbi said that the precept of the fringes is equal to all the other precepts of the Torah (*Ned.* 25a). The Talmud puts it like this: "Seeing leads to remembering and remembering to performing" (*Men.* 43b)).

The fringes are also an identification mark. In mediaeval Europe Jewish people were compelled to wear humiliating badges and articles of clothing. Hertz suggested that the tzitziyot began, at this time, to be an honorable uniform. The badges of the world spoke of contempt. The tzitziyot spoke of God's love for Isra'el, and Isra'el's determination to be faithful and obedient (Hertz, *Numbers* 160). As such it becomes an honorable uniform, diverting attention from the present and visible to invisible and eternal realities.

It is acceptable to make tzitziyot beautiful. By doing this we are adorning not ourselves but God. The Talmud teaches that it is right to "make a beautiful *sukkah* in his honor, a beautiful *lulav*, a beautiful *shofar*, beautiful fringes, and a beautiful Scroll of the Law" (*Shab*. 133b). That is one way we can fulfill the words, "This is my God: I will glorify him" (Exod. 15:2). Obedience to Torah is a joyous service, not an oppressive burden. Therefore we delight to do more than the minimum commanded. We do not just wear fringes; we wear *beautiful* fringes! That is known as *Hiddur Mitzvah*—a concept that means "the embellishment of the commandment."

The *tallit* is the enveloping garment that bears the tzitziyot. It represents God's all-encompassing protection, reminding us that we have a special relationship with the Almighty. As we wear it, we may think of words from the Psalms. "Hide me in the shadow of your wings"; "I will...find refuge in the shelter of your wings"; "In the shadow of your wings I rejoice" (Ps. 17:8; 61:5; 63:8).

Yeshua

Yeshua would certainly have worn the standard four-cornered garment with fringes. Without it he would not have been called up for the reading of Torah. Luke records such an occasion in chapter four of his gospel. The same applies to Sha'ul. He would never have been allowed to stand up in synagogues unless he was appropriately dressed. Their wearing of tzitziyot is not mentioned. Their failure to do so would have been. Remember how the authorities were always on the lookout for opportunities to criticize Yeshua's rabbinical credentials.

"If I can only touch his robe"

The woman had had a hemorrhage for twelve years, and was therefore ritually unclean. For twelve long years she had been untouchable according to Levitical law. Think of the loneliness. Think of the depth to which her self-esteem must have fallen. We do so need to touch and be touched. What a struggle to bring herself to the point of touching the rabbi and making him ritually unclean, thus risking his wrath! See her creeping up behind him, crouching down and touching the tzitziyot on the hem of his long robe. Surely, oh surely, if she just touches the holiest place on the holy man's garment she will be healed, and maybe he will not even notice.

The tzitziyot, however, represented all that God himself is. God had said that looking at them was a reminder of who he was and what he had said. Touching them in trust was touching the source of healingGod himself. "Who touched me?" asked Yeshua. He knew that someone had tapped his power. She was afraid because she ought not to have touched him. He was delighted, because she had reached out in trust. This incident is recorded in Matthew (Chapter 9), Mark (Chapter 5), and Luke (Chapter 8).

For Thought

The wearing of the *tallit* can be meaningful for believers in Yeshua. Dan Juster, an elder statesman of the Messianic Jewish movement, points this out (Juster, 214). He suggests that as the Sh'ma is a call to love the Lord our God, so the tzitziyot are a visual reminder of that call. Sadly, we often find ourselves in the position of the Messianic community in Ephesus. We have lost our first love for the Messiah; we have grown cold toward him (Rev. 2:4). As we place the *tallit* upon ourselves, we have the opportunity to return to our first love, to allow his warmth to rekindle our hearts once again.

Nothing is more calculated to re-awaken love as the reminder of past blessings. This final section of the Sh'ma ends with a reference to the deliverance from Egypt. That national deliverance leads the believer in Yeshua to contemplate his personal deliverance from the bondage of sin. How can we not love him who first loved us, and demonstrated that love at such a cost!

Juster also sees the *tallit* as a symbol of the garment of righteousness. We know that of ourselves we can never achieve righteousness. We can, however, wrap ourselves in the *tallit* and remember that Yeshua clothes us in the garment of righteousness that he alone has the right to own and to give. Truly he has become righteousness for us (1 Cor. 1:30). As Isaiah the prophet foresaw:

> He has clothed me in salvation [*yeshua*],
> dressed me in a robe of *tzedakah*. (Isa. 61:10)

The Messianic doctrine of justification by faith or grace through trust means that as we stand before God he pronounces us not guilty on the grounds of the sacrificial death of Yeshua. God's Holy Spirit then works out that righteousness in our lives. Doctrine alone can be dry and cold. To act out that doctrine can stimulate and revitalize. We need the momentum, and we need the power; God offers us help in so many different ways.

The *tallit*, then, can be more than a visual aid to call to mind God's words and remember to obey them. It can also speak of the finished work of Messiah on the Cross, telling us that we are not alone in the battle against surrounding evil and inner sin. We can love him because our hearts are being softened. We can obey him because he is writing his Torah on those hearts and they are being changed. Hallelujah!

A Prayer

Thank you, Lord, for wrapping me round in a garment of righteousness I have not deserved or earned. Thank you for speaking to me in so many ways about your love and protection. I may look at the hills that offer protection, and the sea that speaks of your power. I will remember, however, that their protection is as nothing compared to the security I have in you:

If I raise my eyes to the hills,
from where will my help come?
My help comes from ADONAI,
the maker of heaven and earth.

He will not let your foot slip—
your guardian is not asleep.
No, the guardian of Isra'el
never slumbers or sleeps.

ADONAI is your guardian; at your right hand
ADONAI provides you with shade—
the sun can't strike you during the day
or even the moon at night.

ADONAI will guard you against all harm;
he will guard your life.
ADONAI will guard your coming and going
from now on and forever. (Ps. 121)

Blessed are you, O Lord our God, King of the universe, who always sustains us, keeps us, and protects us. Blessed are you who softens our hard hearts, warms our cold hearts, and stimulates our unresponsive hearts to love you.

CHAPTER 18

Bless The Lord Who Is Blessed

כרכו את יהוה המברך

Barkhu et Adonai ha m'vorakh

It is customary to surround the recitation of the Sh'ma with *b'rakhot* (blessings), both before and after. These *b'rakhot* were probably formulated by the members of the Great Assembly during the period of the second Temple, after the return from exile. Some may be even older. The Talmud directs that in the morning service there should be two *b'rakhot* before the Sh'ma and one after. In the evening service there are two before and two after (*Ber.* 2a). One should not come casually to the *mitzvah* of Sh'ma without due preparation, or rush thoughtlessly away from it. The *b'rakhot* ensure that things are done with reverence and kavannah.

The *Barkhu*

The *Barkhu* is a call to prayer. It dates back to a time when the morning service was much shorter, consisting only of the Sh'ma and the *Amidah* (the Standing Prayer—the Eighteen Blessings). Today, it serves as a link between the Psalms and songs of praise of the earlier part of the service and the Sh'ma and *Amidah*. The prayer leader calls, "*Barkhu et Adonai hamevorakh*" (Bless the Lord who is blessed). The congregation responds, "*Barukh Adonai hamevorakh l'olam va-ed*" (Blessed is the Lord who is eternally blessed). The leader then repeats the response, lest it seem that he is not associating himself with it.

There are three ways of sanctifying the divine name (*Kiddush HaShem*): by an act of martyrdom; by an act of exemplary moral conduct; by proclaiming faith in him in public prayer. The third of these is usually done responsively; the *Barkhu* is an example.

Following the *Barkhu* is a prayer, spoken by everyone in an undertone:

> Blessed, praised, glorified, exalted and extolled be the name of the supreme King of kings, the Holy One, blessed be he, who is the first and the last, and beside him there is no God. Extol him that rides upon the heavens by his name Yah, and rejoice before him. His name is exalted above all blessing and praise. Blessed be his name, whose glorious kingdom is forever and ever. Let the name of the Lord be blessed from this time forth and for evermore.

Some think that the inclusion of this introductory blessing, with its declaration of God's uniqueness, dates as far back as the Exile. That would seem to indicate that there was a perceived need to reinforce the declaration of God's oneness even at that early date.

Birkhat Yotzer (the Blessing of the Creator)

The first of the two pre-Sh'ma *b'rakhot* in the morning service is *Yotzer*. Here is a blessing of praise to the Creator, who brought forth all things, and who still is acting creatively. This is how it begins:

> Blessed are you, O Lord our God, King of the universe, who forms light and creates darkness, who makes peace and creates all things; who in mercy gives light to the earth and to them that dwell thereon, and in your goodness renews the Creation every day continually.

The *Yotzer* concludes with a plea to the One who continues to order day and night, light and darkness. Surely this reveals a yearning for the days of Messiah:

> Cause a new light to shine upon Zion, and may we all be worthy soon to enjoy its brightness. Blessed are you, O Lord, Creator of the luminaries.

Birkhat Maariv (The Evening Blessing)

The first of the evening blessings also mentions day and night. The Talmud tells us that this theme should be mentioned by both night and day (*Ber.* 11b).

Here is the blessing of God who ordained and controls the rhythms of nature—of day and night, of months and seasons. In ancient times many cultures believed that there were two controlling deities. One was good and ruled the day; one was evil and ruled the night. This *b'rakhah* opposes that belief:

> You roll away the light from before the darkness, and the darkness from before the light; you make the day to pass and the night to approach, and divide the day from the night; the Lord of hosts is your name.

This is God who is the prime mover in Creation, who is in control, and whose right it is to reign supreme as King of his people:

> A God living and enduring continually, may you reign over us forever and ever. Blessed are you, O Lord, who brings on the evening twilight.

Ahavah Rabbah (The Blessing of Great love)

The second *b'rakhah* before the morning Sh'ma begins:

> With abounding love, you have loved us, O Lord our God, with great and exceeding pity have you pitied us.

Chief among the mercies God has showered upon us is his gift of Torah—the laws of life. We acknowledge this gift with great thankfulness, and ask him to make us worthy of it:

> Put it into our hearts to understand and to discern, to mark, learn and teach, to heed, to do and to fulfill in love all the words of instruction in your Torah.... Let our hearts cleave to your commandments.

The blessing concludes with a reminder that God has chosen Isra'el, not by merit but in love. It looks forward to the day when Isra'el will know true peace in her own Land:

> Bring us in peace from the four corners of the earth, and make us go upright to our Land.... Blessed are you, O Lord, who has chosen your people Isra'el in love.

Ahavat Olam (The Blessing of Eternal Love)

This, the second evening b'rakhah, is similar to Ahavah Rabbah. It seems there were two versions of the same b'rakhah, and the talmudic sages could not agree about which was the correct one. At a later date a compromise was reached. One would be said in the morning and one in the evening. This is now the usual practice among western, Ashkenazic congregations.

The difference is significant. Love may seem to be great in the early days of a relationship—but how long will it last? God's love is not only great; it is eternal. In dark days—and there have been many of those—Jewish people have needed to remind themselves that God's love for them is eternal. He has not abandoned or rejected them. He never will; that is not his nature. This b'rakhah, therefore, begins:

> With everlasting love have you loved the house of Isra'el, your people.

The blessing then goes on, as in the morning, to speak of God's gift to us of Torah. The emphasis now is on our responsibility to make Torah an integral part of our daily lives and to rejoice in his words:

> When we lie down and when we rise up we will meditate on your statutes; yes, we will rejoice in the words of your Law...for they are our life and the length of our days....
> Blessed are you, O Lord, who loves your people Isra'el.

Birkhat Geulah (the Blessing of redemption)

The *b'rakhot* after Sh'ma in both morning and evening services deal with the theme of God's deliverance of Isra'el from Egypt. We acknowledge that it was God's hand alone that saved us from Pharaoh, bringing us out from slavery, and opening up the waters of the Sea of Reeds. In both services we recall the Song of Moshe in the prayer entitled *Mi Khamokha* (Who is like you?):

> Who is like you, ADONAI, among the mighty? Who is like you, glorious in holiness, revered in praises, doing wonders?

There is an identification here with the Isra'el of the Exodus. As we remind ourselves in the Passover *seder*, "It is because of what the Lord did for *me....*" So we stand together with all Isra'el— past, present, and future, declaring:

> The Lord shall reign forever and ever.

In the morning, this blessing concludes with a call to God, the Rock of Isra'el, to exercise deliverance again in our times:

> Rock of Isra'el, arise to the help of Isra'el, and deliver, according to your promise, Judah and Isra'el. Our Redeemer, the Lord of Hosts is his name, the Holy One of Isra'el.
> Blessed are you, Lord, who has redeemed Isra'el.

The title "Rock of Isra'el" was used by the prophet Isaiah, speaking of a time in the future when God would "bind up the wounds of his people" (Isa. 30:26, 29). It is a term used in modern Isra'el's Declaration of Independence.

The Talmud teaches that the theme of Redemption should immediately precede the *Amidah*, which itself opens with that theme: "Who...will bring a Redeemer to their children's children for your name's sake" (*Ber.* 4b).

Hashkiveynu (The Blessing for Retiring)

The second *b'rakhah* after Sh'ma is said in the evening only. It is specifically a blessing for the night, and continues the theme of deliverance, with the hours of darkness and danger in mind:

> Cause us, O Lord our God, to lie down in peace, and raise us up, O our King, unto life.... Save us, for your name's sake; be a shield about us.... O shelter us beneath the shadow of your wings; for you, O Lord, are our Guardian and our Deliverer.

There is an additional *b'rakhah* that is not universally used, because it seems to intrude between the Sh'ma and the *Amidah*. It looks beyond the perils of this coming night and the needs of the coming day. One day there will come a time when fear and danger are no more. It will surely happen. We pray that we may live to see it:

> May our eyes behold, our hearts rejoice, and our souls be glad in your true salvation, when it shall be said to Zion, Your God reigns. The Lord reigns; the Lord has reigned; the Lord shall reign for ever and ever: for the kingdom is yours, and to everlasting you will reign in glory; for we have no king but you. Blessed are you, O Lord, the King, who constantly in his glory will reign over us and over all his works for ever and ever.

On *Shabbat*, the conclusion of *Hashkiveynu* is different, perhaps to reflect a yearning that our one day in seven *Sabbath peace* be extended in perpetuity to all Isra'el, both people and Land:

> Spread over us the tabernacle of your peace. Blessed are you, O Lord, who spreads the tabernacle of peace over us and over all your people Isra'el, and over Jerusalem.

Yeshua

The *b'rakhot* that surround the recitation of the Sh'ma in synagogue worship today incorporate a number of themes which were familiar to Yeshua. We see them in his teaching.

The kingship of God is a dominant theme in Yeshua's teaching. From the earliest days of his public ministry he was proclaiming the nearness of the Kingdom of Heaven (Matt. 4:17), the good news of the Kingdom of God (Luke 4:43). The prayer pattern he taught his *talmidim* includes the words, "May your Kingdom come," and ends with this doxology: "For kingship, power and glory are yours forever" (Matt. 6:10, 13). These words surely recall the insertion in the Sh'ma: "Blessed be his name, whose glorious kingdom is forever and ever." However, Yeshua saw that Kingdom, not as a dream of the future, but as a potential present reality. Where God reigns as King in people's lives and communities, there is the Kingdom.

God's nature of love is highlighted in Yochanan's writings— both the gospel and the letters. One of the best-known sayings in the New Covenant Scriptures is John 3:16. Here God's love is seen to be costly beyond understanding. Later we see Yeshua developing that theme: God gave his only Son out of love; that Son will give his own life out of love (John 15:13). The binding of Isaac had pointed the way; God would himself provide the sacrifice. That is love indeed.

Yeshua was always conscious of God's special love for Isra'el. We see his longing heart as he wept over Jerusalem. His words on that occasion recall God's anguished plea to Isra'el spoken through the prophet Yesha'yahu: "If only you would heed my mitzvot! Then your peace would flow on like a river" (Isa. 48:18). He never forgot that it was to Isra'el first that his Father had sent him. When he was angry it was not with Isra'el but with those who were leading her astray with false teaching, human traditions, corruption. His message and his mission were for the world, but they came first to Isra'el and they were couched in terms that were primarily Hebrew. Sha'ul understood this clearly. He is known as the apostle to the gentiles, but wherever he traveled he went first to the synagogue. "To the Jew especially, but equally to the Gentile" comes to us almost as his watchword (Rom. 1:16).

The supreme importance of Torah is another theme in Yeshua's teaching. Contrary to what is taught in many churches, he had not come to destroy Torah, but to complete it (Matt. 5:17). He did not come to make it easier to achieve righteousness. The Sermon on the Mount (Matthew 5–7) makes it clear that he raised the standard even higher, making it harder. He also, however, promised that the Holy Spirit would be available to give the power to achieve those standards. The shame of the Christian Church through the centuries has been that this promise of grace has not been universally accepted. What has been seen—particularly by Isra'el—has been a travesty of true Messianism. So true is this, that the very word "Christian" is distasteful to many Jewish people, even those who believe in Yeshua as Messiah and Savior.

Redemption was the purpose of Yeshua's life and death. The word means "buying back." That is what he said he had come to do, "to give his life as a ransom for many" (Matt. 20:28). He made this plain, to all who understand the Passover ritual, as he gave the third cup, the Cup of Redemption, to his *talmidim* on that last night, saying, "This cup is the New Covenant, ratified by my blood, which is being poured out for you" (Luke 22:20). Kefa pointed out that the price paid for redemption was not silver or gold, but the precious blood of Messiah (1 Pet. 1:18, NIV).

Yeshua was well aware of the value of *shalom* and of his people's longing for it. It was one of the gifts he gave his followers: "What I am leaving with you is *shalom*…my *shalom*" (John 14:27). This was not, however, to be a peace of ease and comfort; his predictions of hardship made that clear. Sha'ul understood what he meant: "Let the peace of Christ rule in your hearts" he advised the Colossians. He followed this with what is perhaps a hint as to how they were to do this: They should let the word of Messiah dwell in them richly, fully (Col. 3:15, 16, NIV). God's counsel is still this, as it was when the Sh'ma was first formulated: If we are to lead godly lives we must know and follow his words.

For Thought

There is a pattern to this arrangement of blessings surrounding the Sh'ma in synagogue worship. We begin by blessing God, who is worthy to be blessed. Remember that the word "bless" is related to that for "kneel." We come, therefore, in an attitude of humility. We are approaching the supreme Lord and King of Creation, the One who stands alone and there is no other. We are privileged to approach because he loves us and welcomes us into relationship with him. We have not earned this privilege in any way. He has given us a tool for the cultivation of that relationship, and that tool is his wordTorah. He is the God who has spoken.

We come, then, to the climactic point in our worship—the reading of the Sh'ma. Everything else leads up to or away from this point. These are the words we must not forget; words that define Isra'el as a community, and individual men and women as members of that community.

As we move on from the Sh'ma, there is, though, no sense of anti-climax. It is time now to think about what God has done for us to make the relationship possible in the first place. We can sum this up in one word, Redemption. He intervened in time and space to deliver Isra'el out of slavery, into freedom and a rich inheritance. We were dependent on him then and we are still dependent on him now. He will not fail us for he is utterly faithful.

We round off this section of the worship service by centering again on God himself. We sing a doxology of praise to the King who reigns forever.

Yeshua valued orderliness in prayer, and he gave his followers a pattern to follow in their private devotions (Matt. 6:6–13). Here again, we see beginning and ending with God's person and glory. There is the concern for the sanctification of God's name and the fact of his kingdom. Then, and only then, come the personal matters: food to eat, sins to be forgiven, protection from evil.

Not all our prayer times will follow the same formula. Perhaps, though, there is a case for orderliness in the devotional life. It is simply not good enough to plunge straight in with my list of needs. I can begin and end with God himself. I can revel in his love. I can, as a believer in Yeshua, meditate on how he has spoken to us in the words of Hebrews chapter 1:

> In days gone by, God spoke in many and varied ways to the Fathers through the prophets. But now, in the *Acharit-Hayamin*, he has spoken to us through his Son. (Heb. 1:1–2).

I may dwell on the uniqueness of Yeshua: God's only Son, the only sacrifice fit to purchase full and lasting Redemption. He is the Lamb of God who alone could deal with the sins of a whole fallen world (John 1:29). This is what the Lord did for me!

Forgiveness must be a major theme in the prayer life of a follower of Yeshua: forgiveness given and forgiveness claimed.

It is fitting also to express my dependence on God; I am his child only because he willed it, because he loves me. I love him because he first loved me. I can lead a godly life only as he enables me; a safe life as he protects me. He is, however, faithful. I can trust him.

A Prayer

Abba, Father! You are the Lord of all, the only, unique King, yet you are my Father. This is a wonder that I cannot understand, I just have to accept its reality. I bless your holy name with my words, and long to sanctify your name with my life. Help me to live according to your will today, doing no less and no more than you ask of me, showing my love for you by the way I live my life.

I am your child only because you made me and you love me. You redeemed me with a price beyond measure. My life is in your hands and I depend upon you for everything I need.

Please, Father, show me where there is wrong in my life. Forgive me and make me clean. I reject any bitterness in my heart, knowing that I must forgive even as you have forgiven me.

It is only with your power that I can live the way I should. I know that power is available because your Spirit lives in me. Help me to use it.

Our God reigns. The Lord reigns; the Lord has reigned. You will reign for ever and ever; for the kingdom is yours, and to everlasting you will reign in glory. I have no king but you. Blessed are you, O Lord, the King, who constantly in his glory will reign over us and over all his works for ever and ever.

FINAL THOUGHTS

Do You Love Me?

The Sh'ma is a declaration of relationship. On the one side stands God—unique, alone, and unrivaled; he is ADONAI, the LORD. On the other side stands Isra'el—the people uniquely chosen by God to be his own *s'gullah,* (his special treasure, Exod. 19:5). What is the nature of the relationship between these two parties? What is to be the bond that holds them together in relationship? How will that relationship be expressed? How will that bond be maintained?

God's Side of the Relationship

The Sh'ma identifies the relationship in the words "ADONAI *Eloheynu* (the LORD our God)." God is not simply *the* LORD; he is *our* LORD! We are bound to him as slaves to a master, as subjects to a monarch. He has the right to posit the relationship in this way because he not only created us, but he also delivered us from slavery in Egypt into nationhood and freedom.

Why did God do this? The answer comes to us in one simple, much abused, word: love. It was not because we were in any way special. We were helpless and weak, like an abandoned urchin. We were unattractive, like a prostitute. We were no better than any other nation, but he loved us. Why? We do not know; we shall never understand.

God has loved us with an everlasting love (Jer. 31:3). The origins of that love cannot be traced, and it will never cease. There will never come a time when he will say, "I do not love you any more." He will never lose patience and declare, "Enough already! I am done with this people!" No. Rather, his cry rings down the ages: "How can I give you up, or surrender you, Isra'el?...for I am God, not a human being" (Hos. 11:8–9). We rightly offer him the blessing of *Ahavat Olam.*

His love to us is also great—great beyond measure. Something has to preserve, repair, and renew a relationship so constantly disfigured by failure and betrayal on our part that something is forgiveness. Hoshea indicates something of the lengths to which God will go in order to offer forgiveness. Yeshua takes the picture much, much further: "No one has greater love than a person who lays down his life for his friends" (John 15:13). So he spoke, and so he did. Jew and Gentile believer alike do indeed rightly offer him the blessing of *Ahavah Rabbah*.

Our Side of the Relationship

What, then, is to be our part in this relationship? How are we to respond to God's great and everlasting love? What does he ultimately desire of his *s'gullah*? The answer comes again in that same simple, much abused word: love. "You shall love the Lord your God." All the words of the Sh'ma following these simply qualify the requirement to love. We are to love God with everything that we are and have. We are to love him whether we feel like it or not. We are to love him with constancy and loyalty. We are to love him when the way is hard and the light is hidden. We are to lay our stubborn will at his feet; that is the nature of real love.

Such love does not come naturally to human beings. God describes the problem in the words he gave to the prophet Hoshea. Isra'el's love, he says, is like "a morning cloud, like dew that disappears quickly" (Hos. 6:4). It is limited, and it fades away under pressure. God's nature is love, but ours is not. For us, love has to be worked at, encouraged, helped, and The Sh'ma gives us some clues about how God himself offers that help and encouragement to the people who call on his name.

God's Words

It was in love that God gave Torah to Isra'el and, through Isra'el, to the world. We may know him as Almighty God; we may know and love him as Redeemer. If, however, we try to go through life with just that basic level of relationship with God, our love will falter at the first hurdle. Love needs to be bolstered by knowledge. The prophet teaches us that without knowledge the people perish; we need to follow on to know the LORD (Hos. 4:6; 6:9).

In God's Word, we shall acquire knowledge *about* him, but more importantly, we shall get to *know* him personally. He reveals himself in all the Scriptures in his holiness and in his love. Without constant, disciplined, and wide reading of the Bible we shall develop an unbalanced picture of him. We shall remain at the level of first love—and first love, as we know, is no basis for a lasting relationship. It must develop and mature, or it disappears altogether. Love matures over time as we get to know one another better. We get to know God better through his Word—through reading it, storing it up in our hearts, doing what it tells us to do.

Fellowship

Fellowship is more than worshipping together once a week. It is keeping company with other believers, and talking together about the Lord. It is being open with one another, caring for one another, noticing and sharing in one another's pain. It is opening our homes, our hearts and our resources. As we make ourselves vulnerable to each other, we are doing what God himself has done for us; we are sharing in his love, and this will reinforce our own love for him.

This fellowship will not exclude our children. We fail them dreadfully, if we do not teach them, both by words and example, about God. They need to know who God is, what he has done, and what he wants to do for them; and they need to learn all this in a context of love. If I love God, I long for my children to know and love him too. This is not indoctrination; it is love.

Communication

All relationships depend on two-way communication. Silence is a killer. As we talk to God, of course we are telling him what he already knows, but that does not mean that prayer is a futile exercise. You may know that your child is hiding something from you. You may even know what that something is, but you will not be happy until he has told you. What is more, you know that he will not be happy either. One secret leads to another, and before you know it your relationship is foundering.

Prayer, like love, does not come naturally to human beings. We need to develop prayer habits, and this takes discipline. What an unpopular word that is. It is definitely not politically correct! Jewish people through the ages have practiced two kinds of prayer. There is the personal, one-to-one, spontaneous reaction to what is currently happening. Then there is the regular, mandatory, structured recital of set prayers, either in synagogue or in private. The practice of laying tefillin reinforces the discipline of regular prayer habits.

Some people have found it helpful to do something physical as a signal to themselves and their families that "This is my prayer time. Do not disturb." I am reminded of Susannah Wesley, who used to cover her face with her apron at these times, and her many children knew better than to interrupt! If you struggle with prayer discipline, why not consider this suggestion. The matter is important. Your love for God will not grow without prayer.

Reminders

The tzitziyot were for Isra'el to look at and remember God's commandments; the *tallit* is a physical sign of God's protection and shelter. Human beings are not good at remembering things we ought to do, and we easily forget good things that have happened to us. We more easily remember grudges and hurts, which we use to justify bad behavior. How can we remind ourselves of what God has done for us and what we should do for him? If I know, for instance, that certain things trigger an unworthy reaction in me, is there anything visual I can set up to stop that reaction in its tracks?

The mezuzah is a sign that this home is the Lord's. All who live here owe first allegiance to him. All who enter should be aware that God reigns here. There are other ways by which believers can make this statement. We need, however, to be aware of the responsibility this places upon us. In today's climate, where believers are a minority, we become marked people.

This is even truer of the marked car. For years my husband would not have a "fish" on his car, because he thought his driving might bring embarrassment to Yeshua! These things can be a help to us, because they remind us how much our way of life affects our witness. If we love God, we do not want to let him down; we long for others to love him too. This is not self-righteousness; it is love.

Do You Love Me?

This is the question Yeshua asked Kefa, that morning on the Galilee beach after his resurrection. Poor Kefa. After those extravagant promises he had failed miserably—not just once, but three times. Three times, therefore, Yeshua posed him the question: "Do you love me?... Do you love me?... Do you love me?" Perhaps in the minds of both Kefa and Yeshua were the familiar words, "You shall love the Lord your God...."

Kefa really did love him now. He had seen the true extent of Yeshua's love for him. He had accepted for himself the forgiveness made available by Yeshua's act of love. He was going to be given another chance, another opportunity not to deny his Lord under pressure. It was an opportunity Yeshua knew he would take. Kefa would not fail in the same way next time: "When you grow old, you will stretch out your hands, and someone else will dress you and carry you where you do not want to go." He would truly come to the point of loving Yeshua with all his heart, and with all his being. Yochanan's comment on these words was, "He said this to indicate the kind of death by which Kefa would bring glory to God" (John 21:18–19).

Kefa was a failure. This failure offered his love to Yeshua and Yeshua accepted that love. A few days later the Torah that came at *Shavuot* married with the power of Pentecost to transform that cowardly failure into a mighty man of God. Then he really began to follow his Rabbi-*Mashiach*. Then he really began to feed the lambs and the sheep. Then he really set his feet on the path that would lead to martyrdom—loving God with all his *nefesh*.

Today Yeshua is asking each of us this same question: "Do you love me? Do you *really* love me?"

Are you dedicated to him enough to love him? Are you prepared to pay the price of love, whatever it might be? Will you nurture that love, however small and weak it seems just now? Will you put him first in everything?

A Prayer

Lord, you know everything about me. You know that I love you. You also know that I am afraid of what this love may lead me into, ask of me, demand of my loved ones. Yet I realize that your grace and power will never fail me when I am put to the test.

Teach me, Lord, how to nurture and grow my love for you, as I let your love for me permeate every corner of my life. You are my Lord and my God. I am yours; do with me as you will.

Blessed are you, O Lord my God, King of the universe, who has loved me with a great and everlasting love, and who stoops to ask for my love in return. I choose to love you with all my heart, with all my being, and with all my resources.

ברוך יהוה המברך לעולם ועד

Barukh ADONAI *ham'vorakh l'olam va-ed.*

Blessed is the LORD who is eternally blessed.

GLOSSARY OF HEBREW TERMS AND CONCEPTS

Acharit Hayamim—"The last days."

Adon Olam—"Lord of Eternity." A song of praise sung near the end of many synagogue services.

ADONAI—"LORD." When written in capital letters, it serves as a substitute for the Ineffable Name of God, the Tetragrammaton.

ADONAI-*Tzva'ot*—"The LORD of Hosts."

Ahavat HaShem—"Love for God."

Ahavat Olam—"Everlasting love." A prayer said before the Sh'ma in the evening service in synagogue.

Ahavah Rabbah—"Great Love." A prayer said before the Sh'ma in the morning service in synagogue.

Alenu—"It is our duty." A prayer said near the end of many services in synagogue.

Amidah—"Standing." Refers to the "Standing Prayer," the eighteen blessings recited regularly in public and private worship. Also known as the *Shemoneh Esreh* (Eighteen Blessings), and the *Tefillah*.

Avinu Malkheynu—"Our Father our King." Used in prayers of repentance on the Day of Atonement.

B'rakhah, b'rakhot (pl.)—"Blessings." *B'rakhot* is also the name of the first tractate of the Talmud.

B'rit Hadashah—"New Covenant."

Barkhu—"Let us bless." The title of the Call to Prayer in synagogue services.

Bar mitzvah, bat mitzvah (fem.)—"Son (daughter) of the commandment." The religious coming-of-age at thirteen, twelve for girls.

Bat Kol—"The Voice of God."

B.C.E. and C.E.. Respectively, these terms stand for "before the common era" (the Jewish alternative to B.C.) and "common era" (the Jewish alternative to A.D..).

Birkhat Geulah—"Blessing of Redemption." A prayer said after the Sh'ma in morning and evening services in synagogue.

Birkhat Maariv—"Evening Blessing." A prayer before the Sh'ma in the evening service in synagogue.

Birkhat Yotzer—"Blessing of the Creator." A prayer said before the Sh'ma in the morning service in synagogue.

Devekut—"Devotion." Refers to the right attitude in prayer.

Diaspora—"Dispersion" of the Jewish people.

Elohim—"God."

Eyn Keloheynu—"There is none like our God." One of the concluding prayers in synagogue services, often sung.

Gemilut Hasadim—"Acts of love."

HaShem—"The Name." A euphemism for God.

Hashkiveynu—"The Blessing for Retiring." A prayer said after the Sh'ma in evening service in synagogue.

Hasid, Hasidim (pl.)—"Pious one(s)." Hasidism was founded in eighteenth-century Russia by the Ba'al Shem Tov. The Hasidic movement emphasizes Jewish mystical tradition, dynastic leadership (the *rebbe*), and joyful devotion to God through prayer, ecstatic worship, and study.

K'tuvim—"The Writings"; the third section of *Tanakh* (the Old Testament).

Kavanah—"Intent" or "concentration." Refers to the attitude required for praying.

K'lal Yisra'el—"All Isra'el."

Kiddush HaShem—"Sanctification of the name of God."

Kohen Hagadol—"The High Priest."

Lulav—The palm branch, carried by worshippers during Sukkot, together with myrtle, willow, and a citron. This is in obedience to Lev. 23:40.

Mashiach—"Messiah, anointed."

Mezuzah—"Doorpost." A small case containing passages of Torah. Placed on the right doorpost at the entrance of homes.

Mi Khamokha—"Who is like you?" A prayer said at synagogue services, quoting from Exodus Ch. 15.

Middat-ha-din—God's attribute of judgment.

Middat-ha-rahamim—God's attribute of mercy.

Midrash—"Commentary."

Mishnah—"Repetition." The code compiled by *Yehudah HaNasi*, c. 200 C.E. The basis of Talmud.

Mitzvah, mitzvot (pl.)—"Commandment" given by God. A good deed.

Modim—"Thanksgivings." A prayer said in synagogue services.

Nefesh—"Soul, life, personality."

Nevi'im—The "Prophets." The second part of *Tanakh*.

Pesach—"Passover." The festival commemorating the Exodus from Egypt.

Ruakh HaKodesh—"Holy Spirit."

Sh'ma—"Hear, listen." The Jewish statement of faith, found in Deuteronomy 6:4–9; 11:13–21; Numbers 15:37–41.

Seder—lit. "Order." Refers to the order of the ritual meal eaten at Passover to remember the Exodus from Egypt.

Shabbat—"[Day of] rest; Sabbath." *Shabbat* is the seventh day of the week (from Friday sunset to Saturday sunset). God commanded Isra'el to cease from work on this day and to assemble for worship (Exod. 20:8–11; Lev. 23:3).

Shaddai—"Almighty." *El Shaddai* (God Almighty) is one of the names of God.

Sh'khinah—The glory of God, which went before the people as a column of cloud by day and column of fire by night (Exodus 13:21). It came upon the Tabernacle at its completion and the Temple at its dedication. Said to be present with God's people when they pray and study Torah.

Shavu'ot—The Festival of Weeks; Pentecost.

Siddur— lit. "Order." Prayer book of Jewish liturgy.

Sukkot—The Feast of Booths, or Tabernacles, commemorating Isra'el's forty years in the desert before entering the Promised Land.

During this period, Isra'el was vulnerable to the elements and fully dependent on God, a reality symbolized by dwelling in *sukkot* (Lev. 23:33–43; Deut. 8).

Tallit, Tallitot (pl.)—Prayer shawl(s).

Talmid, talmidim (pl.)—"Disciple(s)."

Talmud—Complex anthology of Jewish law and the traditions that accumulated around that law, regarded as authoritative in Judaism.

Tanakh—Hebrew acronym (TNK) from the words Torah (Teaching), Nevi'im (Prophets), and K'tuvim (Writings), i.e. the Hebrew Scriptures, or "Old Testament" (see Luke 24:44).

Tefillin—lit. "Prayers." Also the small leather boxes containing Scripture on parchments that are bound to the forehead and upper arm of a Jew during morning prayers (except on *Shabbat* and festivals). The purpose of *tefillin* is devotional (Deut. 6:8).

Teshuvah—"Repentance, turning."

Tetragrammaton—The Ineffable Name of God, composed of four Hebrew letters—יהוה (YHWH).

Torah—"Teaching, direction." The books of Moses / Moshe, the first five books of the Bible.

Tzaddik—A righteous man.

Tzedakah, tzedakot (pl.)—"Righteousness," "righteous deeds."

Tzitzit, tzitziyot (pl.)—The fringe, or tassel, God commanded to be worn on the four corners of the garment (Num. 15:37–41). Worn now on the corners of the prayer shawl.

Yeshua—"ADONAI [the LORD] saves." Yeshua is Jesus' Hebrew name.

Yetzer harah—"The bad inclination."

Yetzer hatov—"The good inclination."

Yihud HaShem—"The unification of God's name."

Yom Kippur—"Day of Atonement." The holiest day of the Jewish calendar; a fast day, the culmination of a ten-day period of repentance and prayer for the forgiveness of sin (Lev. 16; 23:26–32).

BIBLIOGRAPHY

Adler, Hermann. *The Mission of Israel*. From *A Book of Jewish Thoughts*. Comp. J. H. Hertz. Oxford: Oxford University Press: Humphrey Milford, 1920.

Budoff, Barry A. *A Messianic Jewish Siddur for Shabbat*, 1999.

Cohen, A. *Everyman's Talmud*. London: J.M.Dent & Sons Ltd, 1932.

Domnitz, Myer. *Judaism*. London: Ward Lock Educational, 1970.

Donin, Hayim Halevy. *To Pray as a Jew*. New York: Basic Books, a member of the Perseus Books Group, 1980.

Epstein, Isidore. *Step By Step In The Jewish Religion*. London: Soncino Press, 1958.

Friedlander, M. *The Jewish Religion*. London: Shapiro, Vallentine & Co, 1922.

Halevy, Judah. *The Home of Love*, from *The Penguin Book of Hebrew Verse*. Ed. Carmi, New York: T. Penguin Books, 1981.

Hertz, J. H. *The Authorised Daily Prayer book with Commentary*. London: National Council Jewish Education, 1943.

———. *A Book of Jewish Thoughts*. Oxford: Oxford University Press: Humphrey Milford, 1920.

———. *The Pentateuch and Haftorahs—Deuteronomy*. Oxford: Oxford University Press, 1936.

———. *The Pentateuch and Haftorahs—Exodus*. Oxford: Oxford University Press, 1930.

Hirsch, Samson Raphael. *Horeb*. Trans. Grunfeld, I., London: Soncino, 1962.

Ibn Gabirol, Solomon. *In the Morning*, from *Masterpieces of Hebrew Literature*. Ed. Leviant, C. New York: KTAV. 1969.

———. *The Kingly Crown*, from *The Torah*. Plaut, W. G. New York. Union of American Hebrew Congregations. 1981.

———. *The Soul and its Maker*, from *The Penguin Book of Hebrew Verse*. Ed. Carmi, T. New York: Penguin Books, 1981.

Jacobs, Louis. *Theology in the Responsa*. London: Routledge & Kegan Paul, 1975.

———. *Principles of the Jewish Faith*. London: Vallentine. Mitchell, 1964.

————. *Hasidic Prayer*. New York: Schocken Books, 1973.

Jocz, Jakob. *The Spiritual History of Israel*. London: Eyre & Spottiswoode, 1961.

Josephus, Flavius. *The Works of Flavius Josephus*. Transl. Whiston, William. Edinburgh: W. P. Nimmo, Hay, & Mitchell.

Juster, Daniel. *Jewish Roots*. Gaithersburg, Md: Davar Publishing Co, 1986.

Klausner, Joseph. *Jesus of Nazareth*. London: George Allen & Unwin, Ltd, 1925.

Lamm, Norman. *The Sh'ma*. Philadelphia: The Jewish Publication Society, 2000.

Leviant, Kurt. *Alenu*. From *Masterpieces of Hebrew Literature*. New York: KTAV Publishing House Inc, 1969.

Levine, Moses. *The Tabernacle*. London, Jerusalem, New York: Melechet Hamishkan, for Soncino Press, 1969.

Levner, J. B. *The Legends of Israel*. London: James Clarke & Co., Ltd, 1946.

Lipson, Eric. *Uv'lech'cha Vaderech*. London: *The Hebrew Christian*, Summer 1975. London.

Maimonides (Moses ben Maimon). *Mishneh Torah*.

Montefiore, C. G. and Loewe, H. *A Rabbinic Anthology*. London: Macmillan and Co. Ltd, 1938.

Nanos, Mark D. *The Mystery of Romans*. Minneapolis: Fortress Press, 1996.

Newman, Louis I. *The Hasidic Anthology*. New York and London: Charles Scribner's Sons, 1934.

Plaut, W. Gunter. *The Torah*. New York: Union of American Hebrew Congregations, 1981.

Rashi. *Deuteronomy*. Transl. Rosenbaum, M. and A. M. Silbermann, London: Shapiro, Vallentine & Co, 1934.

————. *Numbers*. Transl. Rosenbaum, M. and A. M. Silbermann, London: Shapiro, Vallentine & Co. 1933.

Romain, Jonathan A. *The Jews of England*. London: Michael Goulston Educational Foundation, 1985.

Rossel, Seymour. *When a Jew Prays*. New York: Behrman House Inc, 1973.

Rosten, Leo. *The Joys of Yiddish*. New York: Penguin, 1989.

Scholem, Gershom. *Origins of the Kabbalah.* Ed. Werblowsky, R. J. Zwi. Transl. Arkush, Allan. Princeton: Jewish Publication Society. Princeton University Press, 1987.

Steinsaltz, Adin. *A Guide to Jewish Prayer.* New York: Schocken Books, 2000.

Telushkin, Joseph. *Jewish Wisdom.* New York: William Morrow and Co. Inc, 1994.

Authorised Daily Prayer Book. London: Eyre and Spottiswoode Ltd, 1957.

Hebrew and English Lexicon of the Old Testament. Brown, Driver, Briggs. Oxford: Clarendon Press, 1906.

Jewish Encyclopedia. New York and London: Funk and Wagnalls Co, 1901.

Siddur Lev Chadash. London: Union of Liberal and Progressive Synagogues, 1995.

Deuteronomy Rabbah. Mishnaic commentary on Deuteronomy.

Complete Jewish Bible. Transl. Stern, David H. Jewish New Testament Publications, Inc. Clarksville, Maryland USA and Jerusalem, Israel. 1998.

The Soncino Talmud. Judaic Classics Library. CD-ROM. New York: Davka, 1995.

Other Related Resources from Messianic Jewish Publishers

Complete Jewish Bible, Dr. David Stern
Presenting the Word of God as a unified Jewish book, here is a fresh English translation for Jews and non-Jews alike. Names and key terms are presented in easy-to-understand transliterated Hebrew, enabling the reader to pronounce them the way Yeshua (Jesus) did!

Available in Hardback, Paperback, Blue Bonded Leather, and large print.

Blessing the King of the Universe, Irene Lipson
Transforming Your Life Through the Power of Biblical Praise
Insights into ancient biblical practice are offered clearly and practically. Learning how to bless God elevates all aspects of a person's existence to provide great joy throughout each day. When you start *Blessing the King of the Universe* you will find the peace and joy that come from a renewed relationship with God.

The Voice of the Lord, David J. Rudolph, Ph.D., Editor
Messianic Jewish Daily Devotional
Here are words of encouragement that offer insight into the Jewish Scriptures—both Old and New Testaments. Twenty-two prominent contributors provide practical ways to apply biblical truth.

Kingdom Relationships, Dr. Ron Moseley
God's Laws for the Community of Faith
Focuses on the teaching of the Torah (the five books of Moses), tapping into truths that help modern-day members of the Body. Paul had the Torah in mind when he wrote "all Scripture is valuable for teaching the truth, convicting of sin, correcting faults, and training in right living."

God's Appointed Times, Rabbi Barney Kasdan
A Practical Guide for Understanding and Celebrating the Biblical Holidays
How can the biblical holy days such as Passover/ Unleavened Bread and Tabernacles be observed? What do they mean for Christians today? Provides an easily understandable and hands-on approach. Discusses historical background, traditional Jewish observance, New Testament relevance, and prophetic significance of the biblical holidays.

God's Appointed Customs, Rabbi Barney Kasdan
A Messianic Jewish Guide to the Biblical Lifecycle and Lifestyle
Explains how biblical customs (like circumcision and the wedding) impact both Jews and Christians. Two sections: "Biblical Lifecycle" and "Biblical Lifestyle." Each chapter offers historical background, traditional Jewish observance, relationship to the New Testament, and relevance to Christians.

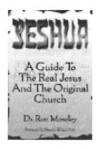

Yeshua: A Guide to the Real Jesus and the Original Church, Dr. Ron Moseley

Dr. Ron Moseley opens up the history of the Jewish roots of the Christian faith. He illuminates the Jewish background of Yeshua and the church and never flinches from his purpose–to show "Jesus was a Jew, who was born, lived, and died, within first century Judaism."

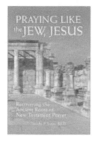

Praying Like the Jew Jesus, Dr. Timothy Jones
Recovering the Ancient Roots of New Testament Prayer
Reveals the Jewish background of Messiah's prayers—particularly their customs and traditions. Historical vignettes transport us into the times of Yeshua (Jesus), so we can grasp the full meaning of his prayers. Unique devotional thoughts and meditations, presented in down-to-earth language, provide inspiration for a more meaningful prayer life.

These books are available through:
Messianic Jewish Resources International
www.messianicjewish.net
1-800-410-7367

Call or write for a free catalog of other related books, messianic music, Judaica, and more.